# Don't Know Much About the Forgotten Coast

## A Beach History

### By J. Kent Thompson

Copyright 2020 by J. Kent Thompson

ISBN 978-1-71670-469-7

Library of Congress Control Number: 2020914172

All rights reserved, no part of this book may be reproduced in *any* form without written permission from the publisher, except by a reviewer who may quote brief passages. Published in the United States by Lulu Publishing.

1st Paperback Edition

This Book is dedicated to

Peri, Claire, Carolina, Holly, Josiah, Eva, William

each will touch a future where I can never go

but my hope is that wherever life may take them

they will always return to seek the solace of the

Forgotten Coast.

# Table of Contents

### Chapter One Where it All Began      1
*The Forbes Purchase*

### Chapter Two The Early Port Cities      7
*St. Marks, St. Marks Lighthouse, Apalachicola, St. Joseph, Rock Haven, Magnolia, Port Leon, Newport, Newport Sulphur Springs.*

### Chapter Three The Early Coastal Resorts      21
*Wakulla Beach, The Seine Yards, Shell Point, Panacea Mineral Springs, Lanark Springs, Lanark on the Gulf.*

### Chapter Four Getting There in Early Times      53
*The St. Marks Railroad, The Old Plank Road, The Gulf Coast Highway, Bloxham Cut-Off, Newport-Perry Short-Cut, Ochlockonee Bay Bridge, Apalachicola River Bridge, The Big Bend Scenic Highway.*

### Chapter Five The Beaches of the Forgotten Coast 63
*Mashes Sands, Ochlockonee Point, St. James Island, Bald Point, Alligator Point, St. Teresa, Cochran-Phillips Beach, Perkins Beach, Wilsons Beach, Summer Camp, Camp Gordon Johnston, Camp Weed-Bay North, Lanark Village, Carrabelle, Eastpoint, Dog Island, St. George Island, The Bob Sikes Cut, Cape St. George, St. Vincent Island, Indian Pass, Cape San Blas, Port St. Joe, Mexico Beach.*

### Chapter Six Getting There Now      141
*Directions and suggestions of places to visit*

# FOREWORD

If you bought this book (by the way, thanks!) it means you want to learn something about the history and development of the beaches and towns of the North Florida coast. This book traces the history of the **Forgotten Coast**. The area supposedly got its name in reaction to a slight from a tourism group that forgot to put information about the coast from St. Marks to Mexico Beach in its publications. In retaliation a group of local businessmen created their own brochure and map calling the area the "**Forgotten Coast**." The name is a registered trademark of the Apalachicola Bay Chamber of Commerce.

The beaches St George Island, St. James Island, St. Vincent Island, Dog Island, St. Teresa, and Wilson's Beach are explored. I look at the early resorts in Panacea Springs, Lanark Springs, Lanark on the Gulf, Wakulla Beach, and Shell Point. Further I will discuss Mashes Sands, Bald Point, Alligator Point, Cape San Blas, and Mexico Beach. The beginnings of the coastal cities of St. Marks, Panacea, Carrabelle, East Point, Apalachicola and Port St. Joe will also be investigated.

First, let's put the area in perspective: A series of four barrier islands make up some of the most prominent beaches of North Florida. Dog Island, St. George Island, Cape St. George Island (also known as Little St. George) and St. Vincent form a protective barrier to the fragile Apalachicola Bay.

To the west of St. Vincent Island is Cape San Blas and Mexico Beach. To the east of Dog Island is St. James Island which contains Alligator Point, Bald Point and St. Teresa. Further east across Ochlockonee Bay are Panacea, Shell Point Wakulla Beach, and St. Marks.

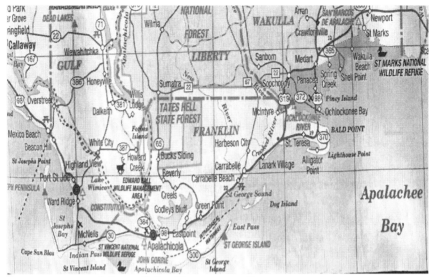

Map of the Forgotten Coast

# CHAPTER ONE – WHERE IT ALL BEGAN

Starting with Ponce de Leon's ships log in 1513 <u>the history of Florida is the oldest recorded history of the new world</u>. While its history dates from then, Florida was not a part of the United States until 1821 when it became a Territory. In 1845 Florida became the 27$^{th}$ state to join the Union. Only sixteen years later it succeeded from that Union to become part of the Confederate States of America. To study its history, one would need to look back at its 250 years in Spain's possession and 16 years in England's. But one must remember, **all** of this land was once owned by the Native American tribes of Apalachee, Creek, and Seminole Indians. The story begins here.

In 1804 the Creeks traded some of their land to the Patton and Leslie Company to cover debts owed to the company. The deal was known as the **Forbes Purchase**. This land was to become, through the years, one of the most valuable properties in North Florida.

From its boundaries came what we currently call the **Forgotten Coast** with its barrier islands of St. George, Dog, St. Vincent, and St. James as well as the cities of Apalachicola, St. Joseph, Carrabelle, Sopchoppy, Crawfordville, St. Marks, Newport, Woodville, Blountstown, and Tallahassee. **The early history of Florida beats within this heartland.**

**Map of the Forbes Purchase - State Archives of Florida**

### The Forbes Purchase

In 1804 the *Paton and Leslie Company* had requested payment from the Indians for all debts as well as losses from theft during Indian raids on their trading posts. In a May 25, 1804 meeting at the Indian village of Cheskatalafa, twenty-four Seminole and Lower Creek Chiefs agreed to transfer 1.2

million acres of land along the Apalachicola River to the company now called *John Forbes & Company* in exchange of cash payments of debts. Originally, Forbes had hoped the Indians would reclaim the land by paying cash for their debt, but instead they later added more land to the deal to offset growing debts. This land transfer was approved by the Spanish government with the stipulation no land transferred would be sold to the Americans. The sale became known as the Forbes Purchase.

The 1804 Forbes Purchase was the largest land grant in Florida history. Three smaller adjacent tracts of land would be added to the original tract in 1811. In total it encompassed 1.5 million acres of land between the Wakulla and Apalachicola Rivers and included the gulf barrier islands to the south and reached as far north as Tallahassee. It encompassed the northwestern part of Leon County, southern portion of Gadsden County, all of Franklin & Wakulla Counties, and all but the northern tip of Liberty County. It was unique in the fact that it was the *only* land grant made by Native Americans that was ever upheld by the U.S. Supreme Court.

By 1816 the influx of settlers and runaway slaves coming into Florida from the Americas soon became too much for the Spanish to handle. Slave owners came seeking their runaways and the Indians preyed on the settlers both in Florida and the neighboring states of Georgia and Alabama. The new American government demanded Spain police their problems as agreed in their October 1795 Pinckney's Treaty (or the Treaty of San Lorenzo). Both sides had agreed to a southern boundary for Florida, to protect navigation on its waters, and not to incite the native Indians to warfare. But Spain, ruling from afar, could not. They had become embroiled in further armed conflicts in Europe and South America and could not spare soldiers to protect their possessions in Florida.

*The John Forbes Company*, sensing the weakness of the Spanish position, and the eventual transfer of Florida to the U.S., decided to sell its holdings rather than try to negotiate a fair price with the Americans. In October of 1817 Forbes sold the land to Colin Mitchel, a Havana, Cuba merchant who held American, English and Spanish citizenship for approximately $135,000.00.

The Americans, also sensing weakness on Spain's part and wanting to secure its southern coasts, told Spain to protect its citizens or trade the land to the United States. After negotiations with U.S. Secretary of State John Quincy Adams, Spain agreed to cede Florida to the U.S. In return the Americans agreed to pay restitution claims of Florida citizens against Spain up to a sum of five million dollars. The U.S. also agreed to give up any claims to Texas.

To look after its citizens and landholders, the Spanish government stipulated that all properties given in land grants *prior* to the Treaty ratification be honored. To honor such a request would have meant that most of Florida would still be held by Spanish citizens. The U.S. resisted this stipulation saying it would have left in place the Alagon, Punonrosto and Vagas land grants, the three largest in Florida. Instead the U.S. agreed to only honor any grants made before the negotiations with Spain had begun on January 24, 1818. This date invalidated the Alagon, Punonrosto and Vagas land grants. While this resulted in favor to the U.S. who looked to recoup their money by selling the lands, they had overlooked one big tract of land, the 1804 Forbes Purchase. Spain formally transferred Florida to the United States through the Adams-Onis Treaty in 1821. In Florida's transfer to the United States it was noted in Article 8 of the Adams-Onis Treaty that:

*All the grants of land made before the 24th of January 1818 by His Catholic Majesty or by his lawful authorities in the said Territories ceded by His Majesty to the United States shall be ratified and confirmed to the persons in possession of the lands, <u>to the same extent that the same grants would be valid if the territories had remained under the dominion of His Catholic Majesty</u>.*

The problem with this clause was it was later contradicted by an 1823 Supreme Court ruling. In *Johnson v. McIntosh* the court had ruled that Indians who had sold land to individuals in Indiana in 1773 and 1775, had no right to sell the land. While they could *possess* it for their use, the European "*discovery*" of America had automatically divested them of the power to dispose of the soil at their own will to whomever they pleased. This "*discovery doctrine*" basically said the land they had long inhabited was now owned by the European discoverers. When England had been in possession of Florida from 1763-83, King George had made a similar ruling. In his "Royal Proclamation of 1763" he barred the purchase of native lands without England's "especial leave and license for that purpose first obtained."

Spain had regained sovereignty over Florida in 1783 through the Treaty of Paris. Spain subsequently signed a 1784 Treaty in Pensacola with the Seminole and Talpuche Indians that promised them <u>*"the security and guarantee of those lands which they hold, according to the right of property with which they possessed them, on condition that they are comprehended within the lines and limits of His Catholic Majesty."*</u>

For the next fourteen years, Colin Mitchel and his associates would argue with bureaucrats, legislators, Governors and judges that the Forbes Purchase was a valid grant that must be upheld by the United States, pursuant to Article 8 of the Adams-Onis Treaty.

The validity of the purchase was first questioned by an 1824 board of land commissioners, and then rejected by an 1830 territorial court in Florida. The case was appealed to the U.S. Supreme Court who postponed hearing it for the next five years. In 1835 the court heard the case and the owners' rights to the Forbes Purchase was upheld in *Mitchel v United States*. The verdict was based upon the Spanish governments 1804 approval and confirmation of the Forbes Purchase when it had occurred.

In its ruling the Supreme Court removed that portion of the Forbes claim to the territory adjacent to the fort at St. Marks, stating it was the property of the United States. It was only because of this ruling that the fort and the city of St. Marks have been preserved in Florida history. The easternmost shore of what is called the **Forgotten Coast** begins here.

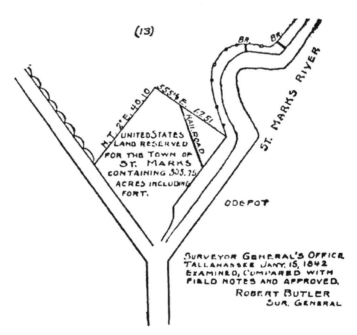

**Survey reserving land for St. Marks and Fort San Marcos de Apalache from the Forbes Purchase as property of the United States**

6

# CHAPTER TWO – THE EARLY PORT CITIES

## St. Marks

St. Marks was once part of the Apalachee Indians territory. They had established the village of *Aute* near the mouth of the St. Marks River. Early Spanish explorers such as Panfilo de Narvaez and Hernando DeSoto ventured into the area, but it was not until 1718 that Captain Jose Primo de Rivera established the first town of St. Marks. He named it after the feast day of St. Mark. Under orders from the Spanish governor of Florida he constructed a wooden fort, the *Fort San Marcos de Apalache,* overlooking the confluence of the St. Marks and Wakulla Rivers. A stone fort was begun on the site in 1739 but took many years to finish. When the United States acquired the fort in 1821 it was alternately used as a garrison and a yellow fever hospital. The city of St. Marks was established in 1828 as a major port on the Apalachee Bay. It was one of five former port communities in the area. Others were Rock Haven (1826), Magnolia (1827), Port Leon (1839) and New Port (1843).

St. Marks has served as a major port to ship cotton, tobacco, naval stores products, and seafood in the early years of Florida's development. Planters traveled in wagons to the port with their goods. In 1834-37 a 22-mile railroad, the first in Florida, would be built from Tallahassee to St. Marks. The original rails were wooden, and the carriages were pulled by mules. In 1856 the rails were replaced by steel rails and the mules by a locomotive. The railway was abandoned in 1983 and the railbed was turned into Florida's first "Rail to Trail" project for hikers and bicyclists. Today St. Marks serves as a port for fuel oil.

During the Civil War, Confederates took control of the fort and renamed it Fort Ward in honor of George T. Ward, Colonel of Florida's 2nd Infantry Regiment who was killed in the Battle of Williamsburg. Before the war he had served on the Florida Territorial Council and was a delegate to the Florida Constitution Convention of 1838 in Port St. Joe. Ward was a major planter in Leon County owning the Southwood, Waverly, and Clifford Place plantations.

**The St. Marks Lighthouse**

The first lighthouse at St. Marks was begun in 1829 and completed in 1831. It is the second oldest lighthouse on the coast of the Gulf of Mexico (Pensacola Light being the first). Legend has it that stones from the old Fort San Marcos de Aplache, six miles away, were used in its construction. In 1842 the original brick lighthouse, threatened by erosion, was torn down and a spot further inland selected for a new lighthouse. It survived the hurricanes that destroyed Port Leon in 1843 and severely damaged St. Marks in 1851.

Originally built to a height of 65 feet, it was damaged during the Civil War and when repaired raised to 73 feet. In 1883 the tower was raised to a focal plane of 82 feet above sea level. The lighthouse was only accessible by water until 193637. A road to the lighthouse was constructed as a project of the Civilian Conservation Corps and built by its African American members. The light, originally lit by kerosene, was changed to electricity in the 1930s and automated in 1960. The Fresnel lens, in service since 1867, was replaced by solar power in 2000. In 2016 The Coast Guard removed their beacon in the lighthouse, and it went dark for the first time since the Civil War. A replica Fresnel light with an LED lamp was relit in the lighthouse on May 2, 2020.

**St. Marks Lighthouse**

## Florida's First Land Boom

After the Supreme Court's favorable ruling, the *Forbes Company* was reorganized as the *Apalachicola Land Company*. What began next was the first of many Florida land booms.

The company hired Asa Hartfield to survey their land. His assessment of their holdings revealed four types of land: hammocks, pine land, swamp and marsh. Only two parcels in the tract were identified as fertile and suitable for agriculture, one along the northern boundary adjacent to Little River and the other on the west bank of the Wakulla River. Later surveys would identify Ochlockonee Bay as a future city site due to its deep-water entrance, but it was never developed. Also noted was Shell Point and the springs and sinkholes in the area. It was said that due to its excellent fishing and healthful air it would be advantageous for sea-bathing and as a summer retreat during the *"sickly season."* It was felt that the land east of the Ochlockonee River had abundant timber resources while the land west of the river had little potential value.

The first four years of sales proved profitable, resulting in the migration of large populations of settlers and a booming local commerce only rivaled by New Orleans, and Mobile. Many of the new arrivals came from Georgia, Alabama, and the Carolina's.

## The Beginnings of Apalachicola

Apalachicola had its start as an Indian village. In 1705 the Spanish built a fort at the mouth of the Apalachicola River, but the area was sparsely inhabited. In the 1750s the area served as a hideout for pirates preying on Spanish treasure ships. Late in the 1700s a trading post was established on

Murder Point (today known as 10 Foot Hole). The town became known as Cotton Town, then Cottonton. When the U.S. took possession of Florida in 1822, the area began to grow. In 1828 the town was incorporated as West Point and then renamed Apalachicola in 1831. When Franklin County was formed from what had been part of Jackson County, Apalachicola became the county seat. By 1835 Apalachicola was the third largest port on the Gulf of Mexico.

Before the *Apalachicola Land Company* could begin selling their land around Apalachicola, they had to deal with squatters. While the company owners had fought in court for their title to the Forbes Purchase land, others had moved onto the property and constructed business's and dwellings with no title at all. With the 1835 ruling upholding the Forbes Purchase, many in Apalachicola thought their squatter claims to the Forbes land would be grandfathered in and they would be granted titles. But this was not the case.

The *Apalachicola Land Company* found a city that had been laid out haphazardly and decided to develop a plan for the town. A street layout mirroring the city of Philadelphia was instituted and the channel from the anchorage to the riverfront wharves was deepened. To protect from fire, business buildings were required to be constructed of brick. To further development, the company donated the streets, squares and a lot for construction of a courthouse. Although they gave first preference to the residents living on the land, many squatters decided to leave rather than pay the prices the company was asking.

Disgruntled former citizens decided to move outside the boundaries of the *Apalachicola Land Company* holdings to St. Joseph's Bay. They formed the city of St. Joseph in 1835 to compete for the river commerce of Apalachicola.

## St. Joseph Founded

St. Joseph took its name from the bordering Bay. Blessed with the deepest port between Pensacola and Key West, the city prospered. The settlers, called "Saints," decided to build a railroad higher up the Apalachicola River from Lake Wimico to the Bay to by-pass Apalachicola. Because the lake was too shallow for deep draft steamboats to pass, a new city called Iona was built at the river terminus of the railroad. The rail line from St. Joseph to Iona was opened in 1839 becoming Florida's first steam-powered railroad.

To protect the shipping, the St. Joseph Lighthouse was built in 1838 at Yellow Bluff (current Beacon Hill) near the entrance to the Bay. The city grew to a population of 4,000. Race tracks, gambling houses, and houses of ill- repute quickly sprang up. St. Joseph's soon was labeled the "wickedest city in the southeast." Visitors included Florida's Governor and legislators as well as the idle rich.

In 1838 Florida's first Constitutional Convention was held in St. Joseph's, not because of its southern charm, but its reputation. Success is sometimes a fleeting visitor and for St. Joseph this proved to be true. In 1840 the railroad shut down due to financial problems. This crippled the transportation lines and the cities commerce. In 1841 a yellow fever epidemic, brought by a crewmember aboard a merchant ship, killed 75% of the town's residents and visitors. Those who survived moved away, some even dismantling homes and moving them back to Apalachicola. In 1844 a major hurricane with huge tidal waters destroyed what was left of the town. Today St. Joseph is but a ghost town of graves.

Apalachicola continued to be a major port only to begin its decline after the Civil War. They could not compete with the new railways that created faster, more efficient means to transport goods. Timber, naval stores, and commercial fishing, coupled with tourism were always prevalent in the area and would become the basis of future economies. The seafood industry has always been a mainstay in Franklin County, but the oyster industry has been the most successful.

The *Apalachicola Land Company* later struggled and went into receivership in the 1860s. It was a 1913 law establishing the Florida Shell Fish Commission that gave the state the right to lease submerged lands and plant oysters that got the attention of the trustees of the *Apalachicola Land Company*. Once again claims to the Forbes Purchase lands were back in court.

In 1923 The trustees of the *Apalachicola Land Company* sued Agriculture Commissioner W.A. McRae over the ownership of submerged lands under navigable and tidal waters in Apalachicola Bay. The trustees alleged they owned the water bottoms as granted under the Supreme Court ruling of 1835. The state claimed they were exercising authority under the Florida Riparian Act of 1856 which gave them title below the high-water mark. The *Apalachicola Land Company* trustees countered claiming title to the water bottoms was part of their land grant. The court studied the applicable laws of Spain and England when they were in control of the land and could not find any instance where the rights to navigable waters were granted to individuals. It held that the rights to public use were always reserved by the sovereign and found that the state, not the former *Apalachicola Land Company*, owned the submerged water bottoms.

Today most of the undeveloped lands of what was the Forbes Purchase are either within the Apalachicola National Forest, owned by the St. Joe Paper Company, or Ag Reserves, a company operated by the Church of Jesus Christ of Latter-day Saints.

## When Cotton was the King

Territorial Florida saw its initial growth in what was called "Middle Florida," an area from the Georgia border to the Gulf, encompassing from the Apalachicola River to the Suwannee River. Owned by wealthy planters from Virginia, Georgia, North Carolina, and South Carolina, the counties of Leon, Jefferson, Gadsden, Madison and Alachua had some of the largest cotton plantations. While they also grew tobacco and sugar, cotton was their chief crop. To get their products to northern markets, five port cities, built from 1826 to 1843 on the St. Marks River, competed for their business and became their lifelines. Rock Haven (1826), Magnolia (1827), St. Marks (1828), Port Leon (1839), and Newport (1843).

## Rock Haven

Rock Haven was a town on the east bank of the St. Marks River below Natural Bridge. In 1828 the town petitioned the 24th Congress to cut a canal through Natural Bridge. Their goal was to extend navigation of the St. Marks River 15 to 20 miles further to better serve the Leon and Jefferson county plantations. The canal was dug, but by the time it was finished the town had been abandoned. When Port Leon was destroyed by a hurricane in 1843 the warehouses in Rock Haven and Magnolia were used to store goods until the town of Newport was built.

# Magnolia

> ## SITE OF THE FORMER TOWN OF MAGNOLIA
>
> Two miles north of this site was located the town of Magnolia, founded in 1827 by the four Hamlin brothers of Augusta, Maine. The Hamlin family had been attracted to the new territory of Florida by the availability of land. The Hamlins chose a site on the St. Marks River which had potential for development into a port town. Because of the lack of overland routes to the north, coastal outlets were particularly important to the settlers and planters of Middle Florida. Magnolia quickly developed into a small but busy port, and in 1829, a U.S. customs house was established there. In the early 1830's, the town had a number of stores and warehouses as well as a bank. Increasing cotton production contributed to Magnolia's commercial growth, but soon the climate and navigational difficulties on the river presented problems for the community. Competition came from the nearby town of St. Marks, and in the mid-1830's the customs house was transferred there. Litigation over land claims in the area also contributed to the decline of the community. Bypassed in 1836 by the new railroad from Tallahassee to St. Marks, Magnolia was gradually abandoned. Today nothing remains of the town except a small cemetery.

Magnolia Historic Marker

Magnolia was located eight miles up the river from St. Marks and two miles from Newport. It was developed by four brothers, John, George, Nathaniel and Weld Hamlin who came to Florida from Maine. They sought their fortunes on the St. Marks River, forming the town on July 4, 1827. It was to be a shipping point for cotton going to northern textile mills. The town prospered with two hotels, 40 houses, a newspaper and bank. Its demise occurred when a mule tram road was built in 1834 from Tallahassee to St. Marks that bypassed the town. Adding further insult, the US Custom house was moved to St. Marks. The brothers tried to continue business by shipping goods down river on barges. When the railroad built a bridge over the river to Port Leon in 1839 it limited the size of vessels that could pass, sounding a death knoll to the town.

> **TOWN OF MAGNOLIA.**
>
> LOTS in the new Town of Magnolia are offered for sale. This place is situated 8 miles from Fort St. Marks on the St Marks' river and 15 from Tallahassee. The river can be navigated to the Town by vessels drawing 8 feet water. The situation is high, dry and healthy; it has two Sulphur Springs in the vicinity, one of which is only 200 yards from the Public Square. They are said to possess great medical qualities.
>
> For further information of Terms &c. apply to J. G. and N. Hamlen, St. Marks, or to Augustus Steele, Tallahassee.
>
> St. Marks, 10th August, 1827—24—tf
>
> N. B. A plain of the town of Magnolia may be seen at this office.

Advertisement for lots in Magnolia

## Port Leon

Port Leon was located on the east bank of the St. Marks River. Established in 1836-7 by former residents of Magnolia, it was an important port for the cotton plantations of Florida and Georgia. Incorporated in 1841, at one time it was the sixth largest town in Florida. It was designated as the first (temporary) county seat of Wakulla County after it was carved out of Leon County in March of 1843. Six months later a September 13, 1843 hurricane and tidal wave destroyed the city. Most of its inhabitants felt the site was too vulnerable to rebuild and moved inland to establish a new town called Newport.

## Port Leon, A Ghost Town Two Miles South
## 1838- 1843

The Tallahassee-St. Marks Railroad was critical to shipping materials from all of what was then called 'Middle Florida' and Southern Georgia. In 1839, Richard Keith Call, president of the Tallahassee Railroad Company, founded the town of Port Leon as the railroad terminus in order to capture the cotton shipping business from the towns of Magnolia and St. Marks. The company had a bridge with two openings, built according to the Town lattice design, erected over the St. Marks River at this location. Businessmen from Magnolia were quick to buy lots, build warehouses, and benefit from the new port city. Freight was no longer loaded in St. Marks.

There were twenty or more houses, a saw mill and grist mill; businesses included warehouses, a hotel, two taverns, a post office and a newspaper. Port Leon, established in 1838, was designated the first county seat when Wakulla was carved from Leon County in 1843. Just a few months later the town was destroyed by a hurricane. The storm swept the railroad bridge up the St. Marks River. Residents boated around the remaining center post for decades thereafter.

After the hurricane the railroad company quickly announced that freight would again be accepted in the St. Marks terminal. The residents of Port Leon moved upstream to establish the town of Newport. All that remains of Port Leon are disturbed lands in the St. Marks National Wildlife Refuge and the railroad bed that is now part of the Florida National Scenic Trail. Today the terminus of the Tallahassee-St. Marks Historic Railroad State Trail is in the town of St. Marks where visitors enjoy the laid-back atmosphere, eco-tourism and great food.

Port Leon Historical Marker

## New Port (Newport)

The town of New Port was established in 1843 after a storm destroyed both St. Marks and Port Leon (the old port). Located three miles upriver, the new city became the second county seat of Wakulla County. The town thrived with the first courthouse of the county being built. An iron foundry and Sulphur springs resort added to its development. Two main hotels were the Daughtery House and the Washington Hotel. A plank road constructed in 1855 connected it with another that went into Georgia. By 1856 there were over 1,500 inhabitants, making it Florida's sixth largest town and the fifth largest port of entry in the state. Stages ran three times a week. A road was later built to connect it with Sopchoppy. Towards the end of the Civil War, Union troops coming upriver for the 1865 Battle of Natural Bridge burned down the cotton warehouses, crippling its economy.

It later became a tourist destination when people seeking the healing waters of the springs came to a hotel built there in 1875. It was said that a part of the book "Uncle Tom's Cabin" was written in Newport. Tourists stayed at the cabins and the Newport Springs Hotel. They enjoyed Millers "Old Swimming Hole" and fishing in the St. Marks River

Postcard of the Newport Sulphur Springs Resort

Newport retained the county seat designation until after the Civil War, but its business's and influence began to wane. It was decided to find a suitable site to build a new town. Noah Posey deeded sixty lots to the county with the cravat that the courthouse be moved to the new location. The new town site was originally called Shell Point but was later renamed Crawfordville after local resident, State Senator, and Secretary of State John L. Crawford.

**Mullet Weathervane Atop the Old Wakulla Courthouse**

Honoring the deal made with Posey, the Newport courthouse was moved to Crawfordville in 1866. The courthouse burned down in 1892 and a new courthouse was built out of heart of pine wood in 1894. It was the last wooden courthouse built in Florida. A hand-carved mullet shaped weathervane of cypress was placed on top of the building. The old courthouse was later moved 500 feet from the center of the city and replaced with a new one in 1949. In 1897 a Dr. Rivers from Waukeenah bought the Newport Springs hotel with plans to open a sanitarium. His brother-in-law B.C. Williams took charge of the hotel for him. Newport's waterborne trade and significance continued to decline with the growth of railroads. During both World War I & II it saw some growth in shipbuilding.

**The Original Ouzts' at the Old Plank Road & Newport Bridge**

**Ouzts' Too- Today**

# CHAPTER THREE - THE EARLY COASTAL RESORTS

## Wakulla Beach

Wakulla Beach on Goose Creek Bay was once the home to Native American Indians for a period between 100 and 800A.D. Bird Hammock, two miles north of Wakulla Beach, contains Indian mounds and shell mittens traced back to the Swift Creek and Weedon Island periods. A hiking trail thru the area today takes one to the Cathedral of Palms, an old growth palm forest, and Shepherd Springs, a canopied 60 to 80-foot pool in the woods. For many years Wakulla Beach was a favorite mullet seine yard for Florida and Georgia plantation owners.

Wakulla Beach was developed in 1915 by Senator Henry Walker Sr and his wife Daisy, they built three successive hotels on the property.

Senator Henry N. Walker

Daisy Walker had a dream of establishing a town called East Goose Creek. A plat of the town was laid out, supposedly the first subdivision ever created in Florida, but never developed.

The first hotel was built in an effort to entice visitors and settlers. A main road called Hotel Avenue was cut to the subdivision (now called the Wakulla Beach Road). The Walkers later made the first hotel their home, and in the 1920s built another hotel closer to the beach. That hotel was destroyed by a 1928 hurricane. Not to be discouraged they built a third hotel in place of the second (pictured below).

**Ruins of the third and last hotel built.**

Daisy Walker died in 1935. In 1949 Senator Walker donated the property to the U.S. Fish and Wildlife Service who added it to the St. Marks National Wildlife Refuge. The hotel was later demolished. Today all that remains on the property is a foundation of the old hotel.

## Wakulla County Seine Yards

The Walkers Hotel at East Goose Creek was well known as a tourist location early in the twentieth century, but it was West Goose Creek that drew the fishermen. The West Goose Creek Seine yard, one of sixteen seine yards located between St. Marks and Turkey Point in Franklin County is one of the area's oldest and longest surviving seine yards. Along with West Goose Creek, only two other locations survived into the modern times; Shell Point and Bottoms. It was at these seine yards where fishermen of old (and some still today) came to fish for mullet, Florida's "money fish." Many of the seine yards were either named after the landowner, the property itself, or the area in which it was located.

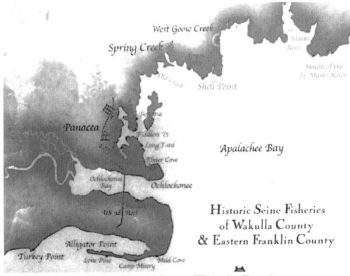

**Scine Yard Map at Wakulla Beach**

The term seine yard applies to an obstacle free area of shallow water off a beach where a beach seine net could be set and then hauled out and the catch processed. A seine net is a wall of webbing supported by a cork line and weighted by a lead line. In the old days, it was constructed of heavy cotton twine of small mesh, so that the fish do not normally gill. A seine encloses fish and as the ends of the net are drawn together the catch becomes concentrated in an everdecreasing area. Usually a 600 to 800-yard seine net would be set from a boat. One end would be anchored on the beach and the other rowed off shore in a semi-circular manner. As the fish would travel along the shoreline they would be enclosed in the net. Once encircled the boat would row back to shore and the net hauled in either by teams of horses or by many hands on the shore.

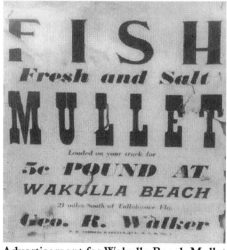

**Advertisement for Wakulla Beach Mullet**

As advertised by the poster, fishermen at the Wakulla Beach seine yard operated a profitable business during the run season. George Walker, son of Daisy Walker even offered the extra service of loading it in your truck. The mullet "run season" lasted from October to December. Mullet would naturally frequent these shallow water areas as they moved east to west along the coastline. Keeping their "right eye to the shore," they moved from West Goose Creek around to Shell Point, Bottoms, Ochlocknee Bay and Turkey Point.

In early Florida, after harvesting their fall crops, the Middle Florida plantation owners would load up their families in wagons and come to the seine yards to catch mullet. They would set up camps and spend their days catching and processing the mullet. The fish would be cleaned then processed by smoking or salting. The fish were then stored in wooden barrels for shipping or storage for later use. Many plantation owners used mullet as a source of food for their slaves. Others would come to barter farm goods in exchange for fish. All in all, it was a festive occasion.

Other seine yards in Dickerson Bay, Smith Creek, Ochlocknee Bay, Shell Point, Alligator Point and St. Teresa also profited from sales. Throughout the first half of the twentieth century the seine yards operated unabated. But new regulations passed in the second half of the century would be the cause of their extinction. From closed seasons, to gear regulations, to an all-out net ban, the seine yards suffered. Today they are but a memory passed down among fishing families of the "good old days."

### Shell Point

Located on the northern edge of Apalachee Bay, one can trace Shell Point's history back to 1528. Explorer Panfilo de Narvaez came here seeking the Indian village of *Aute*. He ended up stranded and had his men build the first ships constructed in America on its shores. They built five barges and departed from the Bay, but only four men of the original expedition of 250 survived.

In 1835 after claims for the Forbes Purchase were settled, the area was surveyed by Asa Hartfield. He made note of Shell Point and the surrounding springs and sinkholes in the area as being good for development. Citing the excellent fishing, he further stated that the healthful air would be advantageous for sea-bathing and as a summer retreat during the *"sickly season."* In his 1837writings about Territorial Florida, John Lee Williams mentions a place of *"pleasant and healthy situation where lots were being laid out to accommodate those who wish to avail themselves of a pleasant summer retreat on the seashore."* A small community sprung up, but a September 1843 hurricane destroyed all the homes, killing the family of Edward Walker who only survived by clinging to a tree.

Shell Point slowly developed, mainly as a retirement community. A.B Taff and Son's Inc. developed the Shell Point Resort, building a motel, restaurant, and marina on the property. The area became a favorite spot for families with young children to come and play on the shallow beach that once served as a mullet seine yard. The restaurant was known for good seafood and the marina gave easy access to the Gulf. By 2000 things began to change, the restaurant shut down, then later in 2001 the marina and hotel closed. After the death of longtime director George Taff Sr., the surviving family members could not agree on how to manage the property going forward. A deal to sell it fell through, and buildings sat vacant. Hurricane Dennis in July of 2005 was the final blow, resulting in the properties being condemned. A yearly sailboat regatta is held here in honor of Stephen C. Smith. Smith, who suffered from leukemia, died in 1974. The proceeds from the race are donated to fight cancer.

**View of the Shell Point Café - 1967**

**The Shell Point Hotel and Marina**

Today Shell Point is a golf cart retirement community. It has a mixture of summer homes, a yacht club, and a trailer park. The beach sand was re-nourished in 2018 with funds set aside from the BP Horizon oil spill and sales tax funds. Native plants, breakwaters, dunes and fencing was installed. The roadway was then resurfaced in front of the beach with improved parking and traffic calming devices. The beach, still a favorite for young families, is maintained as a park by Wakulla County. Swimmers, sunbathers, sailors, and windsurfers come to enjoy the sea breezes of the coastal waters.

## Panacea Mineral Springs

The area was originally called Smith's Springs, named after the four Smith brothers from New York. They had bought the land surrounding the springs and one of them had lived there. Others referred to it as Iron Springs on Dickerson Bay. Indians and early settlers had spoken of the healing properties of the waters, and in 1894 W.C. Tully sought out the springs for his health. The location was hard to find, a large pine tree being the only reference to its location. Smith, suffering from chills and fever, claimed the waters returned him to health. He told others of his experience then cleared a road and built a hotel, founding a town at the springs. He called it Panacea, naming it after the Greek goddess of universal remedy. Many locals resented the name change and still refer to the area as Kings Bay or Ochlockonee Bay.

Tully marketed the local mineral springs waters for their supposed healing properties. The difficulty in getting to the springs due to poor roads and impassable trails, and a reversal of fortune, saw Tully's dream of a health resort fail. By 1897 a Mr. Walker owned the hotel. He then sold it to Bostonian Thomas H. Hall with the cravat that one lot be reserved for him to build on plus the right for he and his family to bathe and drink in the springs. Hall saw an opportunity that locals had not. Many knew of the healing powers of the mineral water, but none had tried to market it on the scale Thomas Hall did.

Hall set about improving the property as a health resort building wharves, walks, and salt and Sulphur bath houses. By September of 1897 he was bottling and selling the mineral water, shipping it all over the United States. In 1901 he built a 150-room hotel, calling it the Panacea Mineral Springs Hotel.

Panacea Mineral Springs Hotel, Panacea, Fla.

Hall then leased the hotel operations to Edwin F. Duke. The rooms offered hot and cold water powered by a windmill and all the modern conveniences. The resort boasted billiard and pool rooms, shuffleboard, telegraph, telephone connections, and a post office. Used as a health spa, it touted the healing powers of its mineral springs. Many came to fill containers with the "healing water's" from the Sulphur spring on the property. The springs were located in a pavilion which housed up to twenty-five pools, each labeled for their different medicinal values. There were pools for liver trouble, kidneys, urinary organs, headaches, stomach disorders, and sore throats to name but a few. Water flowed out of cedar stumps into the bathing pools.

Hotel rooms rented anywhere from $8 to $10 dollars a week. Children over ten were an added $5 and servants and children under ten were charged $2. Visitors would ride the train to Sopchoppy then take a stage to the hotel. A smaller hotel called the Bay View Hotel sat near the waters of Dickerson

Bay. In December of 1900 Duke did not renew his lease and management went to Mr. Hall and Wakulla county businessman Frank W. Duval.

The new managers set about upgrading the hotel and its amenities. A balcony was added to the Bay View for guests to sit and enjoy the gulf breezes. Between it and the Mineral Springs Hotel was a large pavilion. On the pavilion were swings, rocking chairs and a piano. Evening concerts, dances and cake walks were held there for the guests. On Saturday evenings the hotel offered open air oyster bakes and crab boils at Rock Landing. On Sundays a service of sacred music was performed. A ten-minute tram ride took guests to Rock Landing and the large salt water bath house enclosed with fencing.

**Bath House's**

A 31-foot gasoline powered launch the "Mary H" was operated by Captain Deal and was available for coastal pleasure trips. Later a quarter-mile bathing beach was built for women and children. South of the hotel were cottages and to the north were the mineral springs. It was open year-round and boasted some of the best hunting for geese, doves, quail and ducks. Guests also came for the abundant crabs, fish and oysters.

By 1901 a tram road was being built from the springs to Sopchoppy. A temporary sawmill was located near the springs to provide the necessary lumber. The hotel also replaced the windmill with a steam engine to power the water system to the hotel, mineral pool and cottages.

In May the tram road was completed and ready for the summer season. The C.T. & G railroad built two tram cars for use, one for passengers, another for freight. Guests arriving in Sopchoppy could now board a two-mule powered tram car on the tram road for the final seven miles to the hotel. The tram car had metal wheels that rolled over wooden rails and carried about thirty people. Passengers sat on wood benches in a car with no sides. A canvas top and oil cloth curtains were attached which could be rolled down if it rained. The trip took about two hours through the woods and swamp over sand hills and log bridges. Passengers riding through the woods could smell the turpentine oozing from the "cat-face" scarred pine trees. The addition of the tram road also opened the Springs up to wheel-chair bound invalids who could not previously make the rough stage coach ride through the woods. The tram was called "Rapid Transit" because it was faster than walking.

After the summer season of 1901 the partnership of Hall and Duval was dissolved with Hall taking over full operations. The Springs rapidly became popular with norther visitors in the winter and southern visitors in the summer. By 1905 the Hotel was managed by John C. Trice. He improved the tram road, taking out some of the "bumps." He also added a new enclosed tram car and put springs on them to make the ride more comfortable. Due to health concerns Trice turned over management to Mrs. J.L. Morgan in June of 1905, but later returned.

Many began looking to the Mineral Springs as a place for a summer home. Called "Tallahassee's Playground" the Springs prospered. The area offered a healthful location with a lack of malaria, good drinking water, and excellent hunting and fishing. Easily accessible by boat, it boasted a deep channel as well as salt and fresh water swimming. The only drawback in 1906 was the lack of direct access by the railroad. To address the problem Manager Trice leased the transportation business to Mr. Langston and Mr. Roddenberry . They repaired the tram road and added new surries and buggies allowing people to go any way they pleased. The service to the hotel was extended to day or night.

The Panacea "Rapid Transit" Tram Car

Waiting on the Tram Car

By 1908 the hotel had been spruced up with new paint and renovations. The tram cars were now run by power and the Springs pools had been enlarged and cemented with walks leading to them. The Mineral Springs Hotel burned down in the mid 1920s. In 1926 S.S. Brinson developed Panacea Park.

In 1927 a new 30 room two-story hotel was planned. R.H.(Hutch) Gibson, a Tallahassee realtor, saw the value in establishing a town and laid out a town site. He cleaned out the springs and built an ornamental fence around the park buildings and pools. Large arches of stone were built at the entrance to the park. A road was now available to Panacea giving one easy access to the Springs and the coast. The new hotel opened July 4, 1927 and featured a boxing match between Florida champ Bobby Lee and New Orleans native Tommy Quinna. The new hotel also offered two pleasure boats the "Francis B" and the "Marion" for excursions around the coast. A new pleasure pier for hotel guests was also constructed out on Dickerson Bay. The resort soon became better known for its recreation than its health properties, but people still sought the waters to drink.

Both the hotel and the pier would burn down in 1932. By 1935 the road had been surfaced with shell and a bridge was built over the Ochlockonee Bay. This gave further access to the beaches on St. James Island. Once, Panacea had been a mecca for tourists from all over the United States. The depression and opportunities to travel with better roads to other parts of Florida led to the demise of the tourist resort. South Florida, once inaccessible and thinly populated, became the new tourist destination. The property on which the springs sat was owned by Mrs. Sadie Hall Randle, when she died it was sold to A.B. Taff and Sons. Seeking the property mainly for timber and naval stores, Taff proposed having the state or county make the Springs a tourist attraction, but the idea failed. The property went into demise with the Bay View Hotel being was torn down in the 1950s. Today the springs are still visible off the side of Highway 98 in Panacea across from the Wakulla Welcome Center.

## Lanark Springs- Lanark on the Gulf - Lanark Village

William Clark, president of the Scottish Land Improvement Company and the Carrabelle, Tallahassee and Georgia Railroad Company, named Lanark after his home in Scotland. "Lana" means land and "ark" place of refuge. The area has alternately been called Lanark Springs, Lanark on the Gulf, and Lanark Village. Before Lanark was established, the area was called Yeoman Springs.

A rail line used for freight (mainly lumber and seafood) was first completed in the area from Carrabelle to Macintyre, only reaching Tallahassee in 1881. In 1894 the company decided to develop Lanark as a resort to promote their railroad business. The Lanark Inn was built in 1895 by the land development company, principal owners of the railroad. The railroad line made Lanark the most accessible of the early beach resorts and offered people immediate access to the gulf. The resort quickly became a favorite spot for visitors from Tallahassee and south Georgia. Guests came to picnic and swim at the wire enclosed salt water pool bath and enjoy the excellent fishing. The wood burning train was said to be slow enough for one to jump off and pick blueberries along the tracks then get back on.

CT&G Advertisement for the "Elegant Casino/Hotel" in Lanark

The Inn was severely damaged in an August 1, 1899 hurricane, but it was slowly rebuilt. By August of 1901 it was reopened to a larger number of guests, managed by Mrs. Annie Bond, who also operated the St. Teresa Hotel. To increase business, the railroad offered regular Sunday excursions from Tallahassee to Lanark and Carrabelle during the summer season. In 1904 a group of businessmen formed the Lanark Improvement Co. seeking to develop Lanark Springs as a resort. They refurnished and remodeled the hotel installing electric lights, hot and cold baths, steam heat and mineral bathing pools. The developers also gave the town a new name, "Lanark on the Gulf" and offered lots for sale.

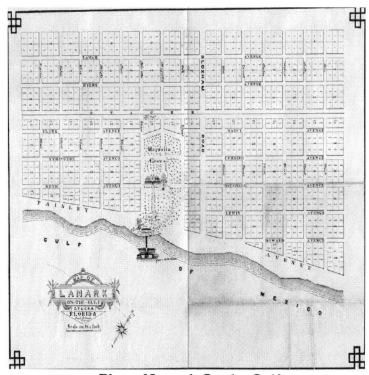

**Platt of Lanark On the Gulf**

The hotel was destroyed in 1907 by a fire that started in the hotel kitchen. Not to be discouraged the developers cleared the property and rebuilt the Inn. It reopened July 15, 1908. Five hundred people from south Georgia and Tallahassee boarded the train to attend the grand reopening and others came by steamer from Apalachicola to the Carrabelle line. The resort continued to attract visitors and by 1911 was serviced by three trains a day. By 1914 the hotel had expanded to 100 rooms.

In September of 1925 the railroad sold the resort to a group of developers. One of the stockholders was Nathan Mayo, the State Commissioner of Agriculture.

The Lanark Inn

The Inn continued to flourish with State Road 10 opened to Panacea providing access to the area to cars. A new dance floor was installed on the pier and a five-piece orchestra was hired to provide music for dancing every night. Besides the Midnight Revelers, the Cooter's Owls, the Florida Nighthawk's, and Son Coleman and his Black Diamonds were featured. Guests at the resort were comfortable in "collar and tie" and drank the Springs mineral water from green bottles. Guest there were far different from the rival "come as you are" St. Teresa crowd.

**MIDNIGHT REVELERS**
5 PIECE ORCHESTRA
NOW PLAYING ON LANARK PIER
**LANARK INN**
On the Gulf of Mexico

DANCING ON THE PIER
EVERY AFTERNOON AND EVENING
DRIVE DOWN DIP. DINE, DANCE
NO BATHING CHARGE TO HOTEL GUESTS
DONT FORGET YOUR BATHING SUITS

Because of increased travel by automobiles the owners had the Pan-American Gasoline Company install a filling station at the Inn's garage. As cars grew more affordable and people began to take to improved roads for travel, the use of railroads for short distance travel declined. The Lanark Inn burned down in 1939 and with it the draw of Lanark as a recreational health spa. When the military took over control in 1942, the remnants of the hotel were torn down and replaced by Camp Gordon Johnston.

# St. Teresa

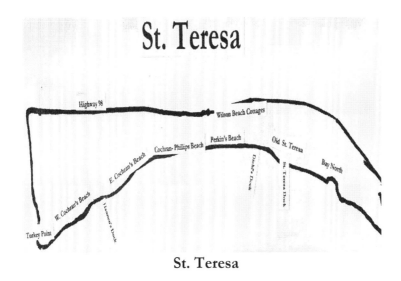

**St. Teresa**

Most people believe that St. Teresa was named after the daughter of one of its later developer/owners, not a Saint, but that may or may not be correct. There **was** a Spanish mission in the area in the 1500s that was named Santa Teresa. Local legend has it that Teresa Leigh "Tee" Hopkins, born September 29, 1856 on St. James Island to Susan and Arvah Hopkins was its namesake. It's more likely that she was named after the Saint who gave her name to the place centuries before. Prior to Hopkins and friends developing a community called Teresa in the 1870s, there were newspaper reports of a September 13, 1843 "great storm" hitting the gulf beach resort area. That same storm was responsible for the destruction of Port Leon, Shell Point, and the Dog Island lighthouse. Meteorologists also reported an August 23, 1851 storm that completely destroyed St. Teresa, *five years before* Teresa Hopkins was born.

Existence of an earlier development is bolstered by an 1874 letter from Dr. Flavius Augustus Byrd to his brother-in-law Judge Gwynn, both prominent Tallahassee residents. He spoke of having gone to the area some 30 years before and picking out a spot to build a cottage, though he did not do so until 1874. Wealthy Tallahassee families looking for a summer resort area closer than Virginia, the Carolinas, or other places in the north, bought lots and built cottages in the newly developed 1870s sea-side resort of Teresa. Byrd further reported the sale of thirty lots at the *"historic"* beach. An 1882 Pensacola Commercial newspaper article referred to the area as St. Teresa, James Island. While others may have referenced the area as Teresa, by 1897 it was known exclusively as St. Teresa.

Mr. Hopkins, along with Governor W.D. Bloxham, General Patrick Houston and Joseph John Williams purchased the land from Governor David S. Walker. In 1873 they platted fifteen lots facing the bay and fifteen more behind them. Some early owners were James D. Wescott, Henry Elliot, Dr. Ben Bond, Matthew Lively, Dr. Randolph, Dr. Pearce, the Lewis family, Fain's, Betton's, Gambles, Gwynn's, Byrd's, Henderson's, Owen's, and Winthrop's.

The area called Old St. Teresa is a two mile stretch between Grassy Point (near the location of the former Episcopal church's Camp Weed - now called *Bay North*) to Stingree Point (which is just east of the former Wilson Beach store and cottages). Westward from there are Perkins Beach, Cochran-Phillips Beach, East & West Cochran's Beach, and Turkey Point.

**General Patrick Houston** was the Adjutant General of the State of Florida, appointed by Governor Mitchell in 1893. He served on the Leon County Commission and in the Florida State Senate, presiding over it in 1887. During the Civil War he was a lieutenant in Gamble's Light Artillery and the Kilcrease Light Artillery. He commanded the artillery battery at the Battle of Natural Bridge against the Union Army forces. His plantation, known as the "Lakeland Stock Farm" was located in today's Capital City Country Club area. He built Fort Houston, what today is called the "Old Fort" in the Myers Park development in Tallahassee. It was meant to be a defense against the Union Army attack on Tallahassee during the Civil War. It was never used, as the battle instead was joined at Natural Bridge.

**Arvah Hopkins** was the owner of Goodwood in Leon County. He married Susan Branch, the sister of Governor John Branch. He developed Teresa on St. James Island, named after his daughter Teresa.

**Arvah Hopkins**

**Teresa Leigh Hopkins** (1856-1903) Was born on St. James Island. She was married to Leon County Sheriff John Pierce. She died in September of 1903, and he just four months later. Both are buried in the St. John's Episcopal Church Cemetery in Tallahassee, Fl.

Teresa Leigh "Tee" Hopkins Pearce

W.D. Bloxham

**Governor W.D. Bloxham** was Florida's thirteenth and seventeenth Governor. As Governor he sold four million acres of state lands in the Everglades for one million dollars to Hamilton Disston in a plan to install canals and drain them.

**Joseph John Williams** served as a state representative from Leon County and was elected speaker of the House of Representatives in 1860. He owned five large cotton plantations in Leon county, among them LaGrange, Chairvoux, Shiloh, Hickory Hill, and Betton Hill.

Traveling to Teresa in the early days was an adventure in itself. One could go by land to the Ochlockonee Bay, traverse it by way of a ferry, then travel by carriage and wagon to Teresa. Another option was to travel by train from Tallahassee to McIntyre and ride a wagon sent Monday thru Saturday by the St. Teresa Hotel, or travel to Carrabelle and take a boat to St. Teresa.

### The Carrabelle, Tallahassee and Georgia Railroad

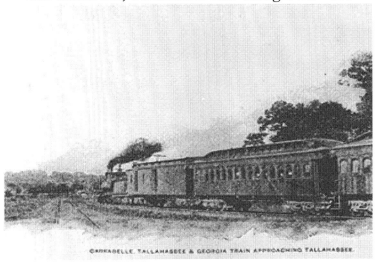

The Carrabelle, Tallahassee and Georgia Railroad was incorporated on January 5, 1891. It serviced the gulf coast of north Florida and southern Georgia. It had earlier been called the Thomasville, Tallahassee and Gulf Railroad and the Augusta, Tallahassee and Gulf Railroad. In 1906 it was sold to the Georgia, Florida and Alabama Railway. Many jokingly referred to it as the Gophers, Frogs and Alligators Railroad.

### Carrabelle, Tallahassee & Georgia R. R.
TIME TABLE IN EFFECT JANUARY 2, 1897.

North Bound—Read down.          South Bound—Read up.

| Miles | No 7 | No 5 | No 3 | No 1 | STATIONS | No 2 | No 4 | No 6 | No 6 |
|---|---|---|---|---|---|---|---|---|---|
| 0 | 10 30 | 6 30p | 5 15p | 11 45a | Lv......Carrabelle......Ar | 9 45a | 10 00a | 4 55p | 6 00p |
| 4.5 | 10 40a | 6 40p | 5 25p | 11 55a | ......Lanark Shop...... | 9 30a | 9 48a | 4 45p | 5 50p |
| 5.0 | 10 45a | 6 45p | 5 30p | 12 00n | ..........Lanark.......... | 9 25a | 9 43a | 4 40p | 5 45p |
| 5.2 | | 7 0 p | 6 10p | 12 45p | ........McIntyre......... | 9 05a | 9 25a | | 5 25p |
| 15.0 | | 7 08p | 6 15p | 12 51p | ........Curtis Mill....... | 8 58a | 9 20a | | 5 20p |
| 10.2 | | 7 10p | 6 20 p | 1 05p | ........Sopchoppy........ | 8 45a | 9 10a | | 5 10p |
| 21.4 | | 7 15p | 6 30p | 1 15p | ..........Ashmore........ | 8 40a | 9 05a | | 5 07p |
| 20.5 | | 7 45p | 6 50p | 1 30p | ...........Arran.......... | 8 10a | 8 45a | | 4 40p |
| 31.9 | | 7 50p | 6 55p | 1 37p | .......Poker's Mills...... | 8 05a | 8 40a | | 4 35p |
| 37.0 | | 8 10p | 7 10p | 1 50p | ........Hilliardville...... | 7 50a | 8 25a | | 4 20p |
| 40.2 | | 8 20p | 7 20p | 2 10p | .......Spring Hall........ | 7 40a | 8 15a | | 4 10p |
| 41.9 | | | | 2 15 | ...........Turner........ | 7 30a | | | |
| 42.0 | | 8 40p | 7 40p | 2 30p | Ar......Tallahassee......Lv | 7 15a | 8 00a | | 4 00p |

Nos. 7 and 8—Lanark Excursions, Sunday only. Nos. 5 and 6—Passenger, Saturday only. Nos. 1 and 2—Daily except Sunday. No. 3—Mail and Express, Sunday only.
Connections: At Tallahassee with trains on F. C. & P. At McIntyre with Oeklocknee river steamers. At Carrabelle with Apalachicola steamers. At Apalachicola with Chattahoochee river steamers. U. S. mail steamer, Crescent City, will leave Apalachicola daily at 7 a. m.; returning leave Carrebelle 12 noon.

S. D. CHITTENDEN,            G. N. SAUSSY,
General Manager.             Passenger Agent.

Railroad Time Tables 1897

Map of railroad connections showing Sopchoppy, Macintyre and St. Teresa Station

46

The Walkatomica

If going by way of the Gulf. One would take the train to St. Marks and then sail by private boat or the "*Walkatomica*.

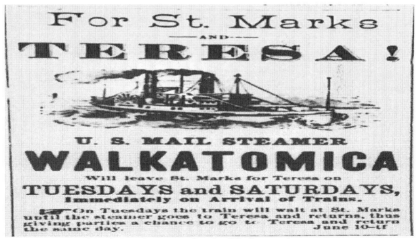

1886 Advertisement for the Walkatomica

The steamboat was built in 1885 by William P. Slusser in Tallahassee. He had it transported on two flat cars to St. Marks then launched it for a maiden voyage to Apalachicola. The vessel was 70 feet long, 13.4 foot- wide, had a draft of 4 feet and was powered by a steam engine capable of 30 mph. It was licensed to carry 50 passengers and commanded by a Captain Phillips. Besides passengers it also carried freight and mail (Teresa was a post office in the 80s & 90s). The name *Walkatomica* was thought by many to be of Indian origin meaning "*the meanest co*w," but Slusser said the name occurred to him in a dream when he was a young man.

Slusser was a major property holder in Tallahassee and around the state in the mid-1800s. While advertising property for sale as part of a real estate company called the Naples Town Improvement Company in 1887, the *Walkatomica* was used to transport people between Naples and Punta Gorda. He at one time ran the City Hotel (or Morgan House), operated a barroom, and also had a general mercantile store (where McCrory's was later located). He built a park for the public to use and called it Slusser Park (located just east of where Franklin Blvd meets Tennessee Street). The park also contained Slusser Pond that was a favorite where the local youth swam. The property was part of the McDougall pastures (where Leon High now sits) before being split by Hwy 90.

When Slusser died the steamer *Walkatomica* became the property of his nephew Charles Blackwell. Blackwell sold it in 1896 to Captain Alexander Breyer and William Berry of Apalachicola. They used it in Pensacola to carry mail and passengers between Pensacola and the navy yard. In October of 1898 it caught fire at her dock in Milton and was destroyed.

In 1889-90 Slusser built a three-story hotel at Teresa said to have cost $100,000. The hotel consisted of a frame building with a long hall running its length with rooms off of it facing the Gulf. *The St. Teresa Hotel* was run in the summertime by Captain Slusser. Mr. Walter Bond bought the hotel in April of 1898 and his wife Mrs. Annie Lloyd Bond was the proprietress, she also ran the popular Jassmine Inn (Bond Boarding House) in Tallahassee. Hurricanes and World War I slowed the development and some of the cottages fell into disrepair. It started coming back to life in the late 1920's.

**Storm Damaged St. Teresa Hotel 1907- Florida Memory**

By 1927 one could reach St. Teresa by car, driving winding dirt roads through the pine forests to the ferry to cross the Ochlockonee River then continuing to St. Teresa. The beaches were always a summer retreat for the mostly Tallahassee families that owned homes there. Many mothers and children would spend the summers while the father's commuted back and forth to work. The 1930s depression and

World War II limited growth of the St. Teresa beach cottages, but in the late 1940s and 50's more cottages were being built.

### Cochran-Phillips Beach

Cochran-Phillips Beach was named after Frank Cochran and his brother-in-law Francis Marion Phillips. Together they operated a naval stores and turpentine still business located in nearby McIntyre. They owned a total of 200,000 acres on St. James Island and later developed the area now known as Cochran-Phillips Beach.

### Perkins Beach

**George B. Perkins**

Perkins Beach was owned by George B. Perkins of Tallahassee. He purchased and developed the Florida Hills Country Club, on land he later sold to the Tallahassee Country Club. That land, once part of the Houston plantation, is known today as the Capital City Country Club.

Some claim Perkin's ownership of the area named for him was by sleight of hand. When representing the sale of Cochran-Phillips properties, he wound up as owner of some of the parcels. In 1933 his wife Margaret Perkins hosted local Girl Scouts at "Camp Margaret" utilizing the cottages of the

Lewis's, Owen's Henderson's, and Van Brunt's. In 1936 Perkins was instrumental in getting a power line constructed from Lanark to the beaches to provide electricity.

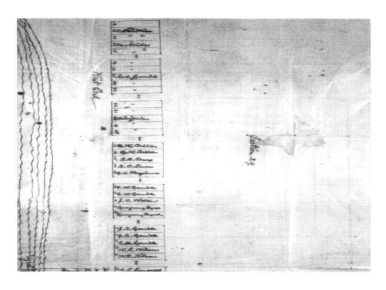

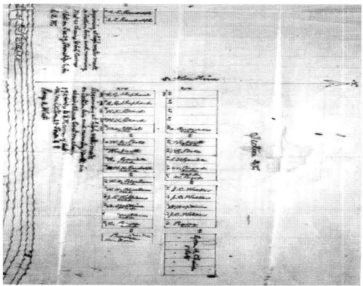

**1870s Plat Maps of Teresa with owners names**

A Forgotten Coast Beach

# CHAPTER FOUR

## GETTING THERE IN EARLY TIMES

The biggest obstacle the early beach-goers faced was how to get there. Prior to becoming a Territory, Florida had few roads and no railroads. The primary mode of transportation over land was by stagecoach, carriage, horseback or wagon. To cross rivers one had to take a ferry. By sea it was by sailboat or steamships.

The port town of St. Marks was key. Growers from Middle Florida and Georgia traveled an early road that connected the territorial capital of Tallahassee with St. Marks. The road was later widened and improved upon by the Tallahassee Railroad Company to become the railbed for the railroad to St. Marks.

The first railroad in Florida, the Florida Central and Peninsular, was a 22-mile line from Tallahassee to St. Marks built in 1834-37. The rails were made of pine with steel straps fastened with hand wrought iron nails. Box like coaches with two benches holding eight people each were pulled by mules.

In 1856 the rails were replaced with steel, and the mules with a locomotive. Two 16-ton locomotives named after area financiers and bankers H.L. Rutgers and General Baily were put into service. In 1858 Edward Houston, president of the P&G and Tallahassee Railroad, offered Sunday excursions to the coast. Passengers could ride the train to St. Marks then get on the steamer *Spray* for a trip to the bay. After a month the effort was abandoned.

Mileage signs at the Sopchoppy Railroad Depot

Early beach goers would ride the train to St. Marks then board the steamship "*Walkatomica.*" The steamship would travel westward over Ochlocknee Bay to the tip of Alligator Point. Once inside the harbor it would dock. The steamer not only carried passengers, but mail and freight. Making three round trips a week, laying over either in St. Marks or St. Teresa at night.

When Florida was ceded to the United States there was only one road of any consequence in the Territory, the King's Road built by the English from St. Augustine to the River St. Mary's. It once extended to New Smyrna but later fell into disrepair. The first American-built road in Florida was from St. Augustine to Pensacola. It was started in 1823 with

$20,000 authorized by Congress. The westward portion was constructed by Captain Daniel E. Burch of the Army Quartermasters Corps. His father-in-law, John Bellamy, constructed the eastern portion. Bellamy built his road sixteen feet wide but left many stumps above the ground, prompting people to call it a "stump knocker" of a road. Named Bellamy's Road, it remained in use until the 1850s. Captain Burch's road west was called Military Trail. Roads generally followed old Indian trails through the pine woods. The trails were widened to six to eight feet and trees were cut down about a foot from the ground. Real road improvements in Florida started in 1915 when the Legislature created the State Road Department. Then in 1916 Congress passed the Bankhead Act that provided systematic federal aid for improving roadways. This began a push to supply rural areas with hard surfaced roads joining cities, towns and villages. In 1923 the longest continuous paved highway in Florida was the 43 miles from Jacksonville to Lake City.

## The Newport Plank Road

To compete with the Tallahassee to St. Marks railroad a group of cotton merchants decided to build a plank road to move their cotton from Georgia to St. Marks. An existing old dirt road built in 1825 southward from the Bellamy road to the fort proved difficult to carry heavy loads in inclement weather and even on good days. Lead by Daniel Ladd, brother-in-law of the founders of Magnolia, he and Joseph Chaires, Green H. Chaires and others, petitioned the legislature for a charter. In January of 1851 the Legislature granted them a charter to build the Florida and Georgia Plank Road, a plank road from Newport to the Georgia line in the direction of Thomasville. The road extended north through Chairs and Miccosukee to just south of the Georgia line. A plank road was made by embedding rails in the ground over boards that were nailed crosswise. Side tracks were graded for turn-off places and drainage. The road bed was 50 to 65 feet wide with no more than a one-foot incline over any 20-foot section. The road only got built as far as Chaires when the money ran out in 1855. A clay road continued on into Georgia and is today called Old Magnolia road. Its purpose was to transport freight to and from St. Marks. This plank road also opened travel to the coastal areas. It was a toll road with cost dependent on number of people traveling and number of animals drawing the vehicle. It was free to walk. Tolls were collected until 1858, the road losing its value after the railroad added a steam engine, taking away the freight business.

## A Gulf Coastal Highway

The Gulf Coast Highways Association held its first meeting in Pensacola, Fl on February 18, 1927 to develop plans for completing the "Florida Loop" of highways down the state to St. Petersburg. Called the Gulf Coast Highway, it was thought it would not only open the area up to tourists but to economic development. North Florida leaders were quick to get behind the idea. Among them were Ed Ball representing the Alfred DuPont estate, who wanted road access to his timber holdings in Northwest Florida. He was joined by W.T. Edwards, Harry Wells, and Dr. Fons A. Hathaway who was chairman of the state road department. Representing the north Florida counties were L.E. Vickery, Bay; Harry Fannin, Franklin; T. H. Stone, Gulf; John A. Scruggs, Leon; and Angus Morrison, Wakulla. To these and other members of the association goes the credit for opening up Florida by making roads available throughout the state.

Local County governments appropriated funds for the work through their counties. The state road department then built the bridges and paved the roads. By 1933 the road was almost complete from Pensacola to Panama City, save for the need to complete some bridges. By 1937 surfacing was completed from Panama City thru Port St. Joe to Apalachicola. From Apalachicola one still had to take a ferry across the bay. In December of 1933 Franklin County voted to issue a bond for $1,500,000 for a five-mile bridge spanning the mouth of the Apalachicola River. The bridge was to be named after Dr. John Gorrie local inventor of the ice machine. Funds had also been designated for a bridge across Ochlocknee Bay. Future plans were for a road to continue along the peninsula to connect with Highway 19 in Perry. Until that leg was completed motorists could only to travel up to Tallahassee on State road No. 10.

Pensacola New Journal Article Nov 12, 1933

The highway was not without controversy In 1936 the original association disintegrated once the roads through to Tallahassee had been completed. Ed Ball and associates had a coastal highway from Pensacola to Tallahassee and saw no need to go further downstate. A new association was then formed to complete the road south and the last link in the highway to St. Petersburg was completed in 1944.

## The Bloxham Cut-Off

Ball's next move was to have a road designated through the forest to Wakulla Springs, saying it was necessary before he could fully develop and promote the springs as a tourist attraction. He received support for his efforts from Braden Ball, publisher of the Pensacola News-Journal in Escambia County who said such a road would cut travel time to Tampa. Leon County Chamber of Commerce head Louis Hill disagreed, saying it would by-pass Tallahassee businesses. Calling it the Bloxham-Newport Cut-off, the road would cutoff of Highway 20 at Bloxham and run to within a mile of the gates of Wakulla Springs, then eventually tie in with the Newport-Perry Highway. Using his political clout, Ball received approval for the road during Acting Governor John's administration in 1953. With the election of Leroy Collins in 1954 the project was cancelled. A long court battle ensued, and it was not until 1963 that the road was approved.

## The Newport- Perry Short-Cut

The next step was to connect the roads to Perry by way of a Newport-Perry short-cut. The short-cut road was called State Road 30 and soon bridges were being built over the Aucilla and St. Marks rivers. Building the road through the Pinhook area of Gum Swamp, construction crews discovered the possible location of the famous Wakulla Volcano which Indians had spoken about centuries earlier. While the road was under construction a significant event supporting the road occurred, the designation of US Highway 98 as a Federally Numbered highway in 1952. It made the road the first federally numbered highway to traverse Florida diagonally. The highways northwestern terminus was Apalachicola and its southeastern terminus West Palm Beach, creating a 500-mile highway. Previously Highway 98 had ended at Apalachicola.

## A Bridge to St. James Island

Though the coast was a popular vacation spot since the late 1800s it was not until the 1930s that a road and bridge made access easier. State Road No. 10 was approved in 1923 and ran from Beechton near the Georgia State line to East Point, via Tallahassee, Crawfordville and Carrabelle. It was extended in 1925 to include the coast to Panacea Springs, St. Teresa, and Lanark. A bridge built over the Ochlocknee River was opened in February of 1927 though there were no roads connected to it. A shell road from Carrabelle was built to the bridge with hopes the same would soon be built from Tallahassee. In 1934 there was only a shell road from Medart to Panacea, by 1936 it had been paved and funds were allocated to continue to the site of the Ochlockonee Bay bridge. The bridge over the Ochlocknee Bay was started in the summer of 1934 and completed in just 14 months. When the bay bridge was opened in September of 1935 it made the beaches easily accessible to all. Until the bridge was constructed one would travel from Medart to Sopchoppy, cross the bridge over the Ochlockonee River then travel a shell road St. Teresa. In 1936 the road from the bay bridge to St. Teresa was finally paved.

## G1A Proposed Linking St. Vincent, St. George and Dog Islands by Bridges

In 1952 A.A. McKethan Chairman of the State Road

Department proposed a 794-mile Gulf Coast Highway from Pensacola to Key West. Calling the road G1A, he envisioned a highway similar to A1A on the east coast. Citing little available revenue, he admitted it was a "dream," but that it should be considered in long range plans using revenue bonds. The proposed route would cross Indian Pass to St. Vincent Island, cross West Pass to Cape St. George then St. George Island. From St. George it would cross over to Dog Island then back to the mainland and U.S. 98 near Carrabelle. From there it would move eastward along Hwy 98 to Crawfordville and Shadeville then to Newport and Hampton Springs to US 98 in Perry. Though there were dreams of a coastal G1A, it never came to pass. When the new St. George Island bridge was opened in 2004 it was designated as G1A until later being designated as State Road 300.

### The Apalachicola Bridge

The Old and the New—The ferries which have been the only means of transportation across Apalachicola bay and a familiar sight to thousands who have ridden them—and a view of a part of the new concrete approaches.

In 1933 Highway 98s eastern terminus was in Apalachicola. To cross the mouth of the Apalachicola river one had to take the single car ferry. Through a $1,500,000 federal bond issue, financing was provided to build a bridge across the river. It was completed and opened on Nov 11, 1935.

Drawbridge Span of Apalachicola Bridge

Souvenir Card from 1935 Bridge Opening

# The Big Bend Scenic Highway (or Byway) Today

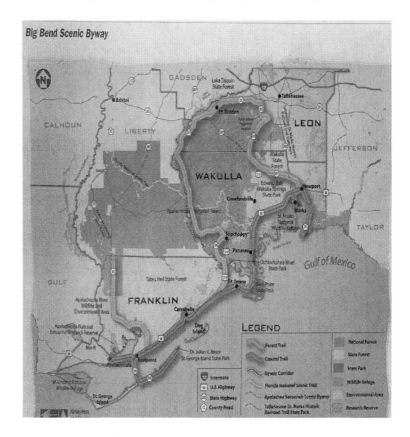

Today one can travel to the North Florida coast by way of the Big Bend Scenic Highway, a 22- mile route that travels through the woods and along the waters of the coast. The only thing that is the same as it was years ago is that the only way in and out is along Highway 98, no interstate connects you to the area. Travelers can visit the beaches, marshes, lighthouses, wildlife centers, hike forest trails, view wildlife, and butterflies, visit parks and museums, and shop local stores in coastal towns along the route. Check out floridascenichighways.com for more information.

# CHAPTER FIVE- THE BEACHES OF THE FORGOTTEN COAST

## Mashes Sands- Ochlockonee Point

Mashes Sands, also known as "The Sands" or "Mashes Island," is a small peninsula bordered by the Ochlockonee Bay and Apalachee Bay. It contains the only white sand beach in Wakulla county. During the Civil War Confederates operated a salt works there. On July 15, 1863 two Union vessels, the USS *Stars and Stripes* and the USS *Somerest* attacked and destroyed the salt works and boilers. In 1984 the state bought two pieces of property from the Harts and McMillians who also donated property to develop as a public recreation area. The location on the end of County Road 372 was for years called Ochlockonee Point.

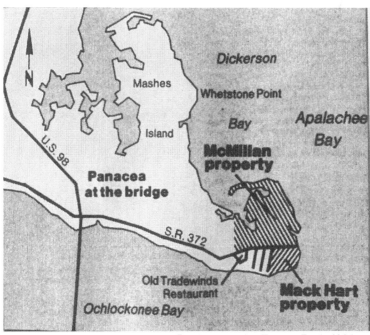

Hart & McMillian Property Designated for Future Park-1984

## James Island- St. James Island

James Island is unique in that many do not realize its size or that it actually *is* an island. It is bordered by three bodies of water; the Ochlockonee and Crooked River's to the north, and St. George Sound to the south. It encompasses the area from the Ochlockonee River bridge to where the Crooked River meets the Carrabelle River in Carrabelle. Bald Point, Alligator Point, St. Teresa, Wilson Beach, Turkey Point, Summer Camp, Lanark Village and Carrabelle are included on the island. The Spanish identified the area in 1527 as La Issa de San Jaume or the Isle of St James. On an 1817 map of Florida the island is noted as part of the Forbes Purchase and listed as James Island. It was only on an 1853 U.S. Coast Survey map of the Florida Panhandle that the name St. James Island appeared. It was the spot for Tallahasseeans to go for vacations. One could either go to the "mountains" or the "Island" also called "Jim Island."

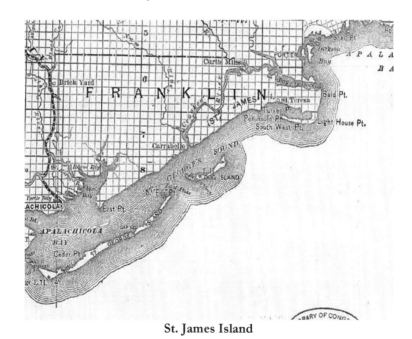

**St. James Island**

## Bald Point

**View of Beach at Bald Point**

Bald Point is located on St. James Islands easternmost point. It sits where the Apalachee and Ochlockonee Bays meet. A 4,800-acre State park offers great opportunities for watching migrating birds and butterflies. The area has served as home to early Florida Indians and turpentine camps . It was used for training soldiers during World War Two. In the 1950s the Southern Dunes Co. planned to develop 800 acres in the area, but it never happened.

Bald Point today consists of privately-owned homes and the 4,000-acre Bald Point State Park located on the easternmost end of Franklin County.

On March 27,1992 a senseless murder occurred on the beach. Two young teenage girls from Thomasville, Ga were brutally murdered. Coming to the isolated beach to enjoy the last days of their high school spring break, they were both shot while sunbathing. Their killer, drifter Robert Neal Rodriguez, had murdered another woman in 1984. At the time of the murders Rodriguez was a part-time janitor at a Tallahassee church. He fled from Florida after being questioned by police when his car matched one seen near the scene of the crime. Rodriguez committed suicide by taking cyanide at a rest stop in New Mexico. He left a full confession of both of his murders near his lifeless body.

## Alligator Point

Indians, evidenced by their burial mounds, lived on Alligator Harbor by 500 B.C. Early explorers to Florida found Indians and an abundance of alligators there, prompting them to name it after the alligators to warn future explorers. It has been said that Alligator Point looks like an alligators tail. Today looking at the stand of pine trees on the tip of the cape one can see what looks like an alligators mouth with teeth. Once called the South West Cape, it is located on the S.E point of St. James Island. The area became a Tallahassee favorite after 1948 when B.K Roberts and his nephew Harry Morrison formed Peninsula Point Inc. and opened it up for development, selling parcels of land.

**View of Alligator Point**

Picnic Tables at Alligator Point Wayside Park

Park was built during Gov. Fuller Warren's Administration

# Wilson's Beach Cottages

Postcard showing Aerial View of Wilson's Beach & Cottages-
Florida Memory State Archives

Postcard showing Wilson's Beach- Florida Memory State Archives

Located on Highway 98, Wilson's Beach was named for its developer William H. "Bill" Wilson in the 1940s. Wilson was president of Wilson Construction and Supply, a company he founded in 1922. He was also a principal developer of St. George Island. The area, a part of St. Teresa, had fifty wood cottages built and painted white to rent to beach goers. With the advent of World War Two, the military confiscated the cottages and used them for quarters for Camp Gordon Johnston officers. A pier and store were constructed, and in May of 1953 a restaurant.

The store was always well stocked with food and beach supplies and provided the only telephone for miles. It also had a gas pump to service vehicles coming from Tallahassee and points north.

William H. "Bill" Wilson

Wilson's Pier

After the war, Wilson's Beach Cottages were used for people seeking summer vacations at the beach. Throughout the fifties and sixties Wilson's Beach was the destination for Tallahassee school parties and teenagers seeking a getaway to party and drink. W.H. Wilson died in October of 1969, the victim of an apparent heart attack at his home. His son took over management of the property and repaired some of the cottages for sale at the price of $17, 500 each. In 1973 Hurricane Agnes dealt a death blow to the pier and many of the cottages had fallen into disrepair. The store was torn down and the pier abandoned. Today the property houses individual homes where the cottages once stood. Only one cottage, Number 6 still stands.

**Interior of the Wilson's Store at Wilson's Beach**

**The Last One Standing – Wilson's Beach Cottage Number Six**

# Summer Camp Beach

Summer Camp Beach covers over 762 acres with four miles of beaches from the end of West Cochran Beach to Turkey Point then west of the intersection of Highway's 319 and 98.

Initial plans called for 499 single-family homes, but a 2008 change in the economy slowed the development. It was part of the St. Joe Co. plan to transform the Florida panhandle.

Distancing themselves from the negative connotation of a panhandler, the company decided to rename the area the "Great Northwest." With timberlands covering Walton, Bay, Gulf and Franklin counties that include 39 miles of coastline, the former timber company turned developer. They built Watersound and WindMark and were a major force in relocating the Bay county airport to attract buyers to their properties.

Choosing to focus on their holdings in Northwest Florida, the company sold 382,834 acres in Bay, Calhoun, Franklin, Gadsden, Gulf, Jefferson, Leon, Liberty and Wakulla counties in 2013 to AgReserves, a company operated by the Church of Jesus Christ of Latter-day Saints.

# Camp Carrabelle - Camp Gordon Johnston

**Col. Gordon Johnston**

The D-Day landing of Allied troops at Normandy on June 6, 1944 is a part of our history. But few know the important part Camp Gordon Johnston, formerly called Camp Carrabelle played in its success.

The camp was renamed for Col. Gordon Johnston, a decorated Army veteran who received the Medal of Honor while serving in the Philippine-American War. He had also served in the Spanish-American War with the Rough Riders and later in World War I.

The camp was opened in September of 1942 to train all phases of amphibious operations to troops and their support groups. The camp was built to model after Camp Edwards in Massachusetts, but with a more intensified training program. One significant difference was the emphasis placed on mental and physical hardening for *all* individuals, not just commandos.

# WORLD WAR II D-DAY TRAINING SITE

In late 1943, Carrabelle Beach and Dog Island, while they were a part of Camp Gordon Johnston, were used by the U.S. Army 4th Infantry Division to train for the Normandy Invasion on D-Day, June 6th, 1944. The Amphibious Training Center had been officially closed, but it was reopened and staffed for the purpose of training for this important mission. Although the troops had trained for over three years, the amphibious training conducted on this site was the last step before shipping out to England for the invasion. On D-Day, the first amphibian infantry assault teams to arrive on French soil were from the 4th Infantry Division at Utah Beach. On June 6, 2000, the Camp Gordon Johnston Association extracted a small amount of soil from this site and delivered it to the National 4th Infantry Division Association to be placed in the Association's monument in Arlington, VA. The U.S. Department of Defense's World War II Commemoration Committee in 1995 named the Camp Gordon Johnston Association an official "Commemorative Community."

FLORIDA HERITAGE LANDMARK
SPONSORED BY THE CAMP GORDON JOHNSTON ASSOCIATION
AND THE FLORIDA DEPARTMENT OF STATE

Historical Marker at Carrabelle Beach

Training at Camp Gordon Johnston- State Archives Florida Memory

Covering 165,000 acres, the camp stretched from Carrabelle to the Ochlockonee Bay. Much of the property was owned by the St. Joe Paper Company. Because of its size, the military was able to train an entire division at once, something not possible before. Isolated and barren Dog Island and St. George Island were used as training landing sites and live-fire ranges. Alligator Point was used for bombing runs. The gunnery range extended from Mud Cove out 20 miles then west 47 miles to the end of St. George Island. Cottages at St. Teresa were taken over by the military as married officer's quarters.

During the war, the camp trained a quarter of a million men. The facilities were crude with most troops living in tents or prefab barracks with sand floors. The mess halls were standup-to-eat affairs and latrines were outdoors. A camp newspaper called *The Amphibian* was printed by the Tallahassee Democrat offices. Added to the crude housing was the heat, snakes, wild hogs, mosquitoes, sand fleas, flies and chiggers. When General Omar Bradley's 28th Division trained there he stated, "The man who selected that site should have been court-martialed for stupidity." Three infantry divisions and two Special Brigades left from the camp to fight in Europe and the Pacific during World War II.

In 1943 the Amphibious Training Center (ATC) was disbanded and replaced with an Armed Service Forces (AFS) training center. The AFS concentrated on harbor craft and amphibian truck (DUWK) or DUCK boat companies headed to the Pacific. Paratroopers from Ft. Benning also trained there. In 1944 the camp became the second largest POW camp in the state, housing 2,500 German and Italian prisoners. It had branch camps at Telogia, Dale Mabry, and Eglin Field's. Camp Gordon Johnston was closed in 1946. In

1948 the camp property was turned over to the War Asset's Administration who sold it to private investors. The investors then began to sell the property piece by piece.

## Camp Weed- Bay North

When the camp closed, Jessie Ball DuPont, owner of the St. Joe Paper Company, contributed a portion of the land to the Episcopal Diocese of Florida.

The Episcopal Church converted their portion of Camp Gordon Johnston to a boys and girls youth church camp. The Reverend Frank Dearing and several youth from the camp built a concrete anchor cross that marks the eastern boundary of St. Teresa. In 1978 the land was sold by the Diocese for $725,000 to Lomax Smith who planned to develop 240 houses on the property calling it Bay North. The county issued him a permit to convert eight A-frame dormitories into duplexes, but county officials, saying it was a mistake, revoked the permit. Smith sued the county, and residents of St. Teresa opposed to the new development, joined the county in the suit. The judge hearing the case ruled for the county, citing concern about the developments impact on the seafood industry. He ordered only 43 multifamily units could be built per the counties zoning law that allows only one unit one per acre. Smith appealed but the zoning restrictions were later upheld.

**Cross at Camp Weed- St. Teresa - Fl Memory**

## Lanark Village

In 1955 Miami investors bought a part of the former Camp Gordon Johnston property from the Lanark by the Sea Corporation for $75,000. The new owners, known as Lanark Estates Inc., purchased the 350-unit housing development that had previously served as military officer quarters. They planned to remodel the government-built apartments, consisting of six apartments under one roof, and sell them as individual homes to northern retirees.

The once famous Springs that flowed like a stream into the Gulf, remained. In 1957 the developers decided to "improve" the Springs by damming it up to enlarge it and create a lake. Using draglines and dynamite, the limestone rocks that formed the headwaters of the Springs were removed. The effort resulted in destroying the Springs and reduced its outflow to a mere trickle.

Original Lanark Village Sign

Seeking to offer homes for retirees living on small pensions, the developers sold homes requiring no down payment with monthly payments as low as $39.50 a month. Promoters offered tour bus trips from St. Petersburg, Clearwater and Tampa to retiree's. They also chartered a tour for retired postal employees from New York. One family that moved to Lanark were the parents of local naturalist Jack Rudloe.

By 1956 there were 157 completed homes with 103 occupied, but the new development was not without controversy. People soon began calling out the developers for misleading advertising. Many of the facilities had not been completed such as the shopping and medical centers or the dock and yacht basin. The ads were used as an example of false advertising before a hearing with Governor Collins by two Lanark residents. The company replied it was an honest mistake but deleted the references in later advertising. Residents complained that there was no telephone service to the community save the one phone in the company office which was closed at night. They also decried the lack of a grocery store and doctor. The company promised they would provide transportation to Carrabelle for groceries and to Apalachicola to visit the nearest doctor.

**Newspaper Ad for Homes at Lanark Village**

Faced with the rising complaints, a stockholder in the company, Frank Newman, bought out the other stockholders and established new management, calling the community Lanark Village. By 1958 the shopping center and docks at the boat basin had been completed. The docks had been built on the deep-water channel dredged by the Army Engineers for use by the former Camp Gordon Johnston. A 40-person bus painted white with "Lanark Village" painted in blue on its sides, was purchased to take villagers on shopping trips and excursions. The development now consisted of 452 homes with more acreage being purchased to build more homes. It was becoming evident that Lanark Village's pioneering effort of a retirement community offering a taste of four seasons was beginning to catch on. Many northern retirees who had had been in the military and had trained in Florida were returning to retire. When the management company went bankrupt in 1961 the residents formed the Lanark Village Association to maintain the community. In 1969, saying they were busier than ever, the Association voted to remove the words "retirement village" from their entrance sign.

**Completed Homes at Lanark Village 1956**

## Carrabelle

Carrabelle was founded in 1877 by Oliver Hudson Kelly who named the town Rio Carrabelle. A railroad connecting Carrabelle to Tallahassee and the Florida-Georgia line was established in 1891 called the C T & G railroad.

## Eastpoint

Eastpoint was settled by David Brown in 1898. They and five other families founded the Co-Workers Fraternity a religious colony that shared their profits from farming, seafood production and lumber. A free ferry service from East point to Apalachicola was opened in 1932.

## Dog Island

Map of Mexico and Florida, 1722 - State Archives Florida Memory

Dog Island is a coastal barrier island 6.8 miles long and a mile at its widest point. It has a natural harbor and an unpaved road extending down most of its length. There is evidence of human presence on the island as far back as 8,000 years ago. Dog Island was "discovered" by the French in 1536 who named it. The French word for dog is Chiens. Its name has one of three meanings. First it resembles the shape of a crouching dog. Second when discovered there were packs of wild dogs roaming the island. Lastly it was used as a drop-off point for common sailors, called sea dogs, to keep them from jumping ship when their ships docked at the mainland.

A 1722 map identified the island as Isle St. Catherine. In a 1763 map of the peninsula of Florida it was noted as Isle de Cani. A 1787 map further identifies **all** the barrier islands as the Isles aux Chiens. For years the island was known as a haven for shipwrecked sailors. Sailing vessels from all over the world anchored in its natural harbor on the lee side of the island dumping ballast in an area known as Ballast Cove. They also took on cargos of lumber and naval stores in Loading Cove (or Shipping Cove.) An 1899 hurricane devastated over 31 ships anchored in the cove. Fifteen were known to have been sunk. The remains of two (one named The Vale) are still there today, uncovered by Hurricane Michael in 2018.

The Island was part of the Forbes Purchase owned by the *Apalachicola Land Company*. On January 5, 1859 it was sold to Benjamin Curtis and George K. Walker by Charles Ellis, receiver for the *Apalachicola Land Company*. Curtis later gained full control of the island. Five acres on the western end of the island was reserved by the United States Government for lighthouse purposes. The Pope family sold the island for $2,400 after World War II. Jeff Lewis and his Tallahassee Aircraft Corporation bought 80 percent of the island from W.B. Miller of Georgia for $12,000 in 1947. The rest of the island was owned by private individuals. Jeff and William Lewis then formed the Dog Island Co.

A Quonset hut on the island (called The Hut) was used to sell snacks and a duplex apartment (the Pelican Inn) capable of housing eight people, was available for overnight stays, extra beds were also available in the Quonset hut. Lewis had designs to develop the island into a seaside resort. At one time looking to build condominiums, a hotel, general store and restaurant. In the early 1950s there was talk of a bridge to the island, but monies were never made available. Lewis was successful in selling lots on the island, improving the 2,400foot private airstrip, and got daily ferry service to the island. Initially electricity on the island was furnished by gas generators, in 1964 Florida Power Corporation installed a power cable to the island. Its water came from shallow wells.

Dog Island Promotional Ad 1958

Lewis had big plans, but he ran into problems with state building and local land-sale codes. In 1968 the Lewis's sold the 200-acre western tip of the island for $140,000 to C. Dubose Ausley, J.C. Gwynn Jr., Julian Smith, Mitch M. Smith and Ben A. Lee. In 1975 a bill was passed by the legislature to form a conservation district on Dog Island allowing greater control over development of the island.

Frustrated with constant fights with the bureaucracy, Lewis sought a buyer for the rest of his island property. In 1978 developer John R. Stocks, a principal owner of much of St. George Island, signed an option to buy Dog Island. Stocks said he intended to build a resort called *Ship Watch Point* with sixty-one houses on five acre lots. In 1979 Stocks option expired, and Lewis began talking with two developers from Miami who offered $4 million dollars for the island seeking to subdivide it into 600 units. The non-profit Nature Conservancy, that buys land for wilderness preservation, also started negotiating with Lewis to buy the island. Lewis decided in 1980 to sell to the Nature Conservancy. The Miami investors sued saying Lewis had broken an agreement to sell to them. A judge later ruled that since there was no agreement in writing with the Miami investor's Lewis was not bound to sell to them. Lewis then sold 1,300 acres to the Nature Conservancy for $2 million dollars. In the sale he got a tax deduction for his charitable contribution. Lewis kept 40 remaining acres for himself. In 1982 the Nature Conservancy, strapped for cash, deeded its 1,300 acres to a trustee of a private trust, the Cuyahoga Trust, set up by New York physician Thomas Roush for $1.35 million. In 1990 islanders got a scare, Roush approached the county asking for the wilderness preserve to be rezoned to allow construction of 63 houses. The County reacted by rezoning the island's residential area to one dwelling per five acres instead of one unit per acre. The Nature Conservancy and Roush then agreed to buy back the property and convey it to the Barrier

Island Trust. The trust was set up by island owners as a public charity to manage the natural areas. They named the 200-acre area The Jeff Lewis Nature Preserve.

## The Dog Island Ferry

**View of Dog Island Ferry Landing and Dock 1976**

Today access to Dog Island is by plane, water taxi or private boat. There was once talk of linking St. George and Dog Islands by a bridge, but a 1985 state and federal law prohibited spending government money on bridges to barrier islands, making it a moot point.

The ferry "*Spica*" had served the island since June of 1955, taking cars and passengers on the three-mile trip across the bay. The old ferry service was discontinued in 1965 and replaced by a government sponsored ferry service. In 1981 U.S. Coast Guard inspectors banned vehicle traffic on the island ferry and only allowed passengers on board, citing excessive rust on the boats deck. In April of 1982 the

Franklin County Commission, citing excessive costs, decided to discontinue ferry service to the island. The decision left the 250 landowners without a way to the island save for aircraft or private boat. Many locals supported the Commissions move. For years they had complained about the monies spent on the ferry saying it was servicing a private island with no public facilities. The Commission then voted to give the Dog Island Conservation District $50,000 of their road construction money plus funds from the sale of the ferry and the ownership of the Tyson Harbor ferry docks on the island and the one in Carrabelle. The ferry *Spica* made its last run to the island on April 30, 1982. The county sold the *Spica* for $44,000 to a company in Boston. It was slated to be used as a tour boat on the harbor. The money received was set aside to buy a new ferry. In August, home owners on the island sued the county over lack of a means to get to the island saying it also affected their property values. To make ends meet the former captain of the *Spica*, Raymond Williams, started a taxi service to the island charging $10 round trip, $6 one way, or $50 to charter the taxi for six persons.

The Dog Island Conservation District took the money from the sale of the *Spica* and bought a surplus military landing craft to transport cars and remove garbage from the island. It was dubbed the "*Elsie M*" by the homeowners. Many decided to bring a used vehicle to the island and leave it there instead of transporting their cars. To get to the island they instead rode a six-passenger boat the "*Ruby B.*" In 2001 longtime ferry operator Raymond Williams retired, leaving visitors to have to resort to a private water taxi service or charter.

Besides the constant threat of hurricanes, Dog Island, along with other barrier islands, is the victim of constant erosion. The east and west ends of the island have been the beneficiary of the shifting sands, but the more populated middle is quickly eroding. Many homes have been lost to the gulf and more are threatened. Dog Islander's take it all in stride. They are used to the biting bugs, critters, snakes and isolation. For the most part they love it, but there is one thing they don't, the annual summer kick-off party called the White Trash Bash. Begun in 1989, the White Trash Bash is held on Memorial Day Weekend. It is a floating drinking party attended by thousands, attracting locals and visitors alike. Because the island is privately owned, revelers anchor in the shallow waters of the cove on the west end staying below the mean high-water line to avoid trespassing arrests. The party features loud music, nudity and lots of booze. Women vie for the title of *Miss Trashy* in an unorganized contest. Dog Island owners say they harm the bird nesting areas and leave their trash. Local and FWC Officers check for impaired boat operators and try to keep the peace.

## Dog Island Lighthouse's

**1851 Dog Island Lighthouse**

The first Dog Island lighthouse was located on its western tip. It was a 50-foot brick tower built in 1839 to mark the middle entrance to St. George's Sound between St. George and Dog Islands. An 1842 storm destroyed the lighthouse keepers house and damaged the lighthouse. A second 40-foot wooden structure was built to replace it in 1843. The second lighthouse was destroyed by an 1851 hurricane. It was replaced by a new 40-foot brick lighthouse in 1851.

During the Civil War the Confederates burned the stairs and damaged the lens to keep it from being used by Union forces. It was repaired after the war, but by 1872 beach erosion had caused it to start to fall. Both the lighthouse and the keepers house were destroyed by an 1873 hurricane. In 1895 it was decided to abandon Dog Island and build a new 103-foot lighthouse near Carrabelle called the Crooked River or Carrabelle Lighthouse.

The lighthouse was electrified in 1933 and automated in 1952. The lighthouse was decommissioned in 1995. A private association rescued it in 1999. The light was restored and relit in 2007.

**1940s Crooked River Lighthouse in Carrabelle**

## St. George Island

A 1753 map identifies the island as St. Georges, the name is repeated again in a 1776 map of the Southern British Colonies. It was supposedly named St. Jorge after the Spanish Saint Jorge the Dragon Slayer by early Spanish explorers. Other say that its name was derived from the English Saint George whose cross is prominent in both the National and Union flags of England. The island was only accessible by boat. In the 1800s, when Apalachicola grew into a major port, there was a hotel built on St. George for travelers who came to Apalachicola, traveling to the hotel by boat. It later deteriorated and was abandoned. From 1890 to 1922 the steamer *Crescent City*, piloted by Andrew Wing, offered round trips from Apalachicola for 50 cents every Tuesday and Friday nights. Passengers would ride the Carrabelle Tallahassee - Georgia railroad to Carrabelle to board the vessel to Apalachicola then dock at St. George Island where Wing had built a wharf and boardwalk.

St. George was originally 28 miles long. In 1957 it was divided by the dredging of the Bob Sikes Cut to allow quicker passage of vessels to the Gulf. As a result of the dredging a nine-mile island called Little St. George was created on the west end. To the east remained a nineteen-mile St. George Island.

For the purpose of tracing principal ownership of the island one must start with the 1804 Forbes Purchase when it was included in land ceded from Creek and Seminole Indians to pay outstanding debts to the Paton, Leslie & Company. The first titled owner was the John Forbes & Company 1804-1817. A succession of owners followed; Richard Carnochan & Colin Mitchel, 1817-35, Apalachicola Land Company 1835-66, George Hawkins (receiver for Apalachicola Land

Co.)1866, Thomas Orman (Little St George 1861) George Sinclair/William Sinclair (1866-1/3 of main island,) Horace H. Humphries and heirs 1881-96, Edward Porter (Little St. George 1894), Dan & Alma Neel (St. George Island 1896-1900), Paul & F.R. King (St. George Island 1900-02), Paul King (St. George Island 1902), W.F. Farley & W.E Montgomery (1905-10).

While there were many owners, there were only a few owners who actually developed the island; George W. Saxon & the St. George Island Co. (1910-13), George W. Saxon (1913-21), William Lee Popham (1921-35), Clyde Atkinson and Bill Wilson 1935-71, John Stocks, Gene Brown-(Leisure Properties)1971-81, St. George Plantation-Gene Brown

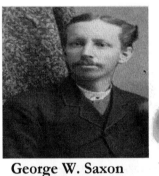

George W. Saxon    William Popham

W. H. Wilson    Clyde W. Atkinson

**George W. Saxon** was a dry goods store owner who began a private bank in his store in 1889 loaning money to farmers. In 1895 he chartered the Capital City Bank in Tallahassee. He was a Tallahassee real estate developer and an early developer of St. Teresa, Lanark and St. George Island. Saxon bought the island in 1910 for $19,600. He and the St. George Island Co. built a hotel called the *Club House* on the bay side of the island near the old wharf boardwalk and leased out the turpentine rights, but they failed to make much money. He took over sole control of the island in 1913. Fifteen to twenty houses were soon surrounding the boardwalk and tourists came to stay in the hotel. Saxon laid out a subdivision, but it never developed as he expected, and it was later sold for delinquent taxes. In 1917 he offered William Popham the rights to sell lots on the island, which Popham did with much enthusiasm and promotion. In 1921 Saxon sold St. George Island to William Popham for $35,000.

**William Popham** was probably one of the most colorful owners of St. George Island. He was an evangelist, poet, writer, gifted Chautauqua speaker, developer, entrepreneur and the self-declared "Oyster King." He used the royalties from his novels as equity to purchase the island. Popham's vision was to develop the island and the surrounding oyster beds. In 1920 he created a co-op called the Oyster Growers Cooperative Association. His plan was to raise and ship oysters to markets around the country. He also started a newspaper called the Oyster Farm News to promote his business. Popham sold shares in his company throughout the United States offering great rewards. Ever the promoter, he mixed his sales pitches with his poems. Investors buying a membership were told they would see the oyster farm produce over sixteen thousand barrels of oysters resulting in a members monthly income of $1,300. He quickly sold over 1,000 shares. Popham grew more confident in his sales ability and changed the goal of the co-op to include lots on St.

George Island. An investor would share in the returns from the oyster leases as well as own a lot. He called his plan the Million Dollar Bond plan. Popham was part promoter part huckster, he renamed the 10-room hotel calling it the *Breakers* and opened a restaurant on the bay side of the island, promising a thousand room hotel there in the future. He also rebuilt the wooden boardwalk where prospective buyers could walk across the island. He got a newspaper to print a story about the fabulous bridge to the island when none existed. He spoke of plans for a game preserve and a health resort.

**A map of Popham's plan for St. George Island and the Oyster Bottom Leases**

It was his use of the mails that brought him trouble. State Shell Fish Commissioner T.R. Hodges alerted federal authorities. Popham was dragged into court charged with mail fraud concerning his oyster leases and methods of advertising St. George Island, as well as the illegal sale of oyster leases. The legal battle raged for a couple of years before going to trial. In January of 1925 Popham was convicted and sentenced to four years in prison. Popham put his properties in what was called the Popham Trust Estate. During his time in prison the island property changed hands and Little St. George was sold. Popham was released after serving two years in federal prison and began promoting his new Cultivated Oyster Farm Corporation much like he had done before. He spoke of creating a powdered form of oysters made in cube and tablet form. He also developed a drink called "Oyster Nip" to rival the soda drinks of the day saying it was nutritional *and* tasty.

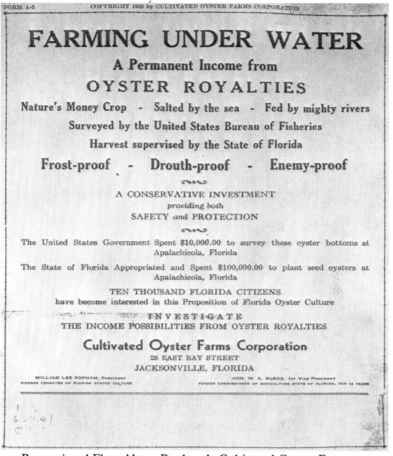

Promotional Flyer About Popham's Cultivated Oyster Farms Corporation

A leech infestation of the oyster beds in 1935 crippled Popham's plans, and soon he was back in debt. To add to his woes, he was once again charged with mail fraud. Popham went to trial with his lawyers Senator William C. Hodges and Clyde A. Atkinson. Popham was acquitted, but had to turn over St. George Island, mortgaged at $8,000, to his lawyers to pay his attorney fees.

### Clyde W. Atkinson, W.C. Hodges and William H. "Bill" Wilson

Twice the lawyers sold the island, first to a hunting club for $25,000 then again in 1942 for $35,000. But it reverted back for lack of mortgage payments. At the beginning of World War II, the island was leased for the duration as a bombing range. It has been said that some of the trees on the island became so imbedded with bullets from strafing runs they could not be salvaged for pulpwood.

Senator Hodges died in 1940 and his widow sold her interest in the island to her brother William H. Wilson. The government paid the owners for use of the island, but it was barely enough to cover taxes. One good result of the military bombing was the discovery of an 18-foot layer of packed oyster shell covering several acres of marsh on a point of the island. The shell was used by the developers to pave 18 miles of road on the island. Many early travelers on the island remember these shell "washboard" roads that would cause your car to vibrate and shake as you drove over them.

In 1951 Clyde Atkinson and William Houston "Bill" Wilson platted out lots in the first four-and a half-mile subdivision and began to sell them. Because of the lack of access to the island, the sales were slow. A beachfront lot went for $2,500 financed at $25 a month. Many families in Tallahassee bought lots only to later resale them for minimal or no profit or turn them back to the corporation due to financial difficulties making the payments. The developers approached Bryant Grady "Pat" Patton, local State Representative and owner of the Apalachicola Fish and Oyster Company for assistance. They were seeking a way to increase their holdings and add to the Franklin county tax rolls through developing St. George Island. What they needed was easy access to the island. In

1951 Patton helped sponsor legislation to allow toll bridges to be built to Florida's barrier islands.

**Bryant Grady "Pat" Patton**

Getting to the island was a challenge. Ferry service had been established in 1955 to both St. George and Dog Islands by Franklin County. But one had to plan their trip to and from the island based on the ferry schedule. Once on the island there were few amenities, no air conditioning, television, or garbage service, and the water tasted like Sulphur. Many owners of homes on the island today would be surprised to find out some of their lots once were used as trash dumps. On the plus side, you could drive cars on the beach and dunes and there was great surf fishing. In the fall the island offered excellent duck and dove hunting.

**Early View of Public Beach- Current Location of Blue Parrot and the Restored Lighthouse**

Initially there were only five full-time families on the island. The first permanent residents were retired Master Sargent Walter C. "Sarge" Cassel and his wife, WAC Corporal Delores Cassel. Both disabled veterans, they moved to the island in September of 1956 from Okinawa after being discharged. Sarge was a Franklin County special deputy, Chief of the volunteer fire department, and civil defense coordinator for St. George. He also was a jack -of-all- trades, repairing appliances, and building and renting dune buggies to ride on the beach. Delores was active in the community, historian of its civic club, and wrote a column for the local paper called *"I'm Sirius."*

## Island Bridges Proposed

Representative Bryant Patton's act allowing toll bridges to be built to barrier islands was instrumental in a push to provide linking bridges to St. George and Dog Islands and the mainland in Carrabelle. In August of 1951 Franklin County voters overwhelmingly approved the project. The St. George bridge would start at Cat Point and be four miles long. The Dog Island bridge from Carrabelle to the Island would be 1 ½ miles. To pay for the bridges, which if East Pass was also bridged, would cost around $5,000,000. The county would collect tolls, receive a per cent of the money for which lots were sold, and use surplus gas tax money to cover the building costs. Owners of the islands agreed to offer public beaches and room for wayside parks.

The County Commission passed a resolution stating their intentions were to build both bridges, but the St. George bridge was given priority if only one bridge could be financed. Dog Island owners protested saying a bridge to their island would be shorter and cheaper, plus the island was twenty miles closer to Tallahassee. The St. George Island owners countered saying their island was bigger and held more potential revenue. Both islands would also be required to have a landing strip (Dog Island already had one). Principal owners of Dog Island Jeff Lewis and Ivan Monroe also expressed concern about the current shortages of steel and concrete and the tying up of gas tax monies for a possible 30 years for just one bridge to St. George. To provide dollars for a Dog Island bridge the owners attorney asked that 50% of the gas tax monies be reserved for a future bridge to Dog Island. The Commission moved forward, contracting with a company to do surveys, but cold water was thrown on their efforts by the State Road Board. The Board said they would not approve the use of surplus gas tax monies until they had conducted their own surveys of the feasibility and soundness of the projects.

## Bridge Efforts Stall

For a while it looked like no bridges would be built. Plans were slow developing and the idea of borrowing money to build a bridge by issuing bonds soon cooled, especially when engineers produced a study that estimated the cost to be $6,400,000. Such a cost dashed any hopes of paying for the bridge with tolls and Franklin county gas taxes. Soon talk turned to getting private financing or building a bridge that did not have to meet the rigid standards required by bond lenders. Those ideas were also abandoned. It became evident that the chances of building a bridge were minimal until there was enough development on the island to sustain a flow of traffic great enough to produce enough toll revenue to pay for it. To speed the process, the developers of both St. George and Dog Islands pushed for a ferry service to the islands.

## The St. George and Dog Island Ferry's

In an effort to get development of the islands moving, Patton introduced a bill that would provide funds from property taxes for bridge construction and ferry service to the islands (if approved by local voters). Franklin County Commissioners then passed a ferry service resolution in July of 1953 . They asked the State Road Department to allocate $177, 200 in secondary road funds for a ferry service from the mainland to the islands. If approved, they hoped to have the ferry service in operation by the summer of 1954. The plan was to have two ferries. One from Cat Point on the mainland to the north side of St. George. The other would travel from Carrabelle to Tyson's Harbor on Dog Island. Of the monies, $155, 200 would be used to buy two 12 car ferries and build ferry slips and access roads on both the mainland and the islands. The additional $22,000 would be used to maintain and operate the service for the first year. In August of 1953 the State Road Department approved the Franklin County request.

Developers of both St. George and Dog Island, looking to the promise of ferry service, began developing roads on the islands. Efforts to develop the islands were not without controversy. An employee of the State Road Board, former Senator T. Drew Branch, was suspended after attempting to bribe the owners of St. George Island for property. Branch reportedly told them a six-mile road on the island would be built if they agreed to sell to a person he would name later, a two and a quarter square miles of island property for $36,000. If they refused, he threatened to shut down work on the ferry slips. The owners reported the bribe attempt and Branch was later indicted. Fast forward to 1956 and Branch, while still under indictment, was elected as Senator from Liberty County. The indictment was later quashed.

In March of 1954, acting on Franklin Counties request, the Road Department received legal authority to buy a 10-car ferry boat for service between the islands. By June construction of the ferry slips was underway and one ferry had already arrived. The "*Spica,*" a 9-car ferry had been purchased for $50,000 and had been brought down from New York harbor. A second 9-car ferry the "*Sirius*" was also bought for $55,000 and used temporarily in Nassau and Duval counties on the Buccaneer Trail. In late December of 1954 ferries being used in Tampa until the sky-way bridge opened, were freed up. That allowed the ferry "*Sarasota*" to be transferred to Mayport in Duval county and the "*Sirius*" to leave Duval county and join its sister ship the "*Spica*" in Franklin county.

**Ferry Boat Spica**

In April of 1955 the State Road Department announced they were ready to provide ferry service to the islands, as soon as public demand justified it. The ferry slips and approach roads had been built and the developers were building roads on the islands. Ferry rates were to be $1.50 for car and driver and 50 cents for each passenger or pedestrian round trip. The "*Spica*" had already been put to use in hauling construction materials to the islands. Because the "*Sirius*" was temporarily assigned in Duval county, the "*Spica*" would be alternated between the two islands, St. George Island one week, Dog Island the next. A small passenger boat also alternating between the two islands was to be used for pedestrians.

The "*Spica*" began operating in June of 1955. In July they reported their biggest four days with 1,800 passengers and 202 cars visiting the islands. In September of 1955, the "*Sirius*" finally arrived but was used as an alternate due to limited service and funds. In October a new ferry schedule utilizing the two ferries was set. Use of the passenger boat service was discontinued in September of 1956, and by April the Franklin county commission asked the State Road Department to discontinue service to Dog Island and offer a seven day a week ferry to St. George. At the time it was running five days to St. George and two days to Dog Island. Dog Island owners protested.

In May of 1957 the state decided to get out of the business of running the ferries. They entered into a lease with the developers where they would operate the ferries seven days a week instead of the current five. The lease called for four trips a day to St. George and two a day to Dog Island. If the developers wanted to increase the trips they could do so at their option. The developers planned to use the "*Spica*" for Dog Island and the "*Sirius*" for St. George. An unexpected glitch occurred when Senator T. Drew Branch entered a bill in the senate to limit the road revenue funds to operate the ferries. This was the same person who had been indicted for trying to bribe the St. George developers years before. Mrs. Bryant Patton, now the Representative for Franklin county vowed to kill the bill when it reached the House, calling it "vindictive and spiteful legislation."

## The Ferry Boat's and Their Captains

The two ferries were named after two heavenly bodies, *Sirius* the Dog Star, the brightest star in the sky, and *Spica* the luminary of Virgo. The *Spica* was built in 1949 and the *Sirius* in 1950, both were identical. Bought secondhand from Sunrise Ferries in New York City, they had been used to make the eight-minute run across the Hudson River. They were sixty-five feet long by forty feet wide. Each was powered by two 671 GM diesel engines. The engines were connected to eight Browning "V-belt" drives that turned the propellers. The ferry required a minimum of five and a half feet of water to operate. They had a tunnel running down its center which enclosed a drive shaft. A propeller and rudder were located on each end of the ferry which made them difficult to steer. Designed to hold nine cars, they sometimes held as many as twelve depending on the size.

When the developers leased the ferries from the state they took over hiring the crews, collecting fares, paying operating costs, and maintaining insurance on the ferries. George Bradford, bookkeeper for the SGI Gulf Beaches Inc. was responsible for hiring the crews and daily business operations. A business office was located on St. George Island above the Island Inn store that was run by Fred Hill.

The Captains of the ferry boats were special boatmen. Captain Marion Wing and Engineer Buddy Robinson were the first pilots on the Spica. When Robinson left, Joe "Snookie" Barber took his place, becoming a Captain when Wing later left the ferry. Milton Kelly and his brother, and Raymond Williams also operated the Dog Island ferry, Ned Ferguson served as engineer. When the *Sirius* was put into service Captain Carol McLeod and Engineer David Merchant were on board, Seaborne Jackson also acted as a captain. Barber later became the engineer on the *Sirius*. In July of 1960 Barber became a Captain with Joe Hathcock and Leon Derringer as his engineers. Captain McLeod left the ferry in 1965 before the bridge opened. Barber stayed for a few months after the bridge became operational until the *Sirius* was sold.

After a run across the bay the crews would wait forty-five minutes at the slip for fares then load up and return to the mainland then repeat the same process on the mainland. In the summertime six trips were made then reduced to four after Labor Day until spring. The developers were insistent that the trip schedules be kept with the only exception being the last runs on Sundays. No one wanting to leave the island was to be turned away. This often led to the ferry making more runs, and since Florida had not yet gone to daylight savings time they were often run in the dark of night. A oneway ticket cost 75 cents for a car and driver with an extra twenty-five cents for each additional occupant. Cars would line up at the ferry docks and when the ferry arrived the engineer would collect the fares and guide the cars on board. Cars were loaded along each side first then the middle isle was filled. If smaller cars like a Volkswagen or Nash Rambler were in line they would move them to the front of the loading line. They would put them on along the sides and then bounce them into smaller spaces along the side rails thereby allowing more than nine cars on board. The maximum it could carry in such a manner was twelve.

### Captain Carroll McLeod

Mr. Carroll McLeod was one of the earliest captains of the St. George Island ferry. Before piloting the ferry, he used to run the movie projector at the theater in Apalachicola. He also was very adept at electronics and operated a repair shop. Realizing he would soon be out of a job; he left the ferry three months before it ceased operating to take a job at the government Vitro site on Cape San Blas.

Ferry Boat "Sirius" Captain Carroll McLeod

Cars on the Ferry "Spica" – State Archives, Florida Memory

Captain Joe "Snookie" Barber (L) celebrating his first run as Captain of the "Sirius"

## Captain Joe Barber

Joseph Wesley "Snookie" Barber was born in Apalachicola and lived in the area most of his life, leaving only to go into the Navy in World War II, and later to commercial fish in Pensacola. He got the nickname, "Snookie," from his brother to whom he had returned the favor calling him "Butch." He explained years ago, that everyone had a nickname. After ten years of commercial fishing for snapper and grouper which took him away from his growing family, he realized he either "had to get rid of the boat or his wife." Returning from Pensacola, he and his wife, Erma, raised five children in a home he had bought on Apalachicola Bay. He lived in the same house for forty-four years. It was only in the early 2000s that he sold it and moved to Carrabelle.

"Snookie" was originally hired as an engineer on the St. George ferry in 1960, working with Captain McLeod. With the retirement of Captain Marion Wing, who ran the second crew, Barber finally got his chance to become a captain. He then hired Joe Hathcock to work as his engineer. I met with Captain Barber at his home in Carrabelle to learn more about him and the St. George Island ferry. I asked him to tell me about his time running the ferry and sat with him for hours as he reminisced.

He said that the captains and mates on the ferry always considered themselves "goodwill ambassadors" for the island. They were always willing to talk with their passengers and let their kids come up in the pilot house for the ride across the bay. Vacationers met the first ferry every morning to buy a newspaper from the rack Snookie had placed aboard so they could stay up with the news. Frequently passengers would give them produce from their gardens or money to thank them for their courtesies. Often it came in handy for Captain Barber to have some extra dollars or food when raising a family of five.

If the ferry broke down and people had already come to the docks expecting to get to the Island, Snookie arranged for a friend in East Point to take them to the island on his personal boat. He told the car owners to give him their keys and he would bring their cars over when the ferry was repaired. True to his word, he and his mate would then load the cars and take them across, parking at the landing for the owners to pick up later. Summer times were always the busiest. The biggest day Snookie ever had consisted of a total of 86 cars and 375 people. He once transported a house that had been cut in half to be reassembled on the island. The largest load, however, was one of the ferry's last runs when he brought a loaded semi-truck, a dump truck full of gravel, and three cars.

Snookie said he'd had seen a lot of things and learned a lot about people running the ferry. One of his most embarrassing moments happened when a woman came running down the dock as he pulled away from the island and shouted for him to bring her some Kotex. He was temporarily flustered but soon regained his composure and shouted back, "Do you want regular or king size?"

Once he took a man over to the island who had told him to be sure to save a spot for him on the last ferry as he had to get back to town that night. When it came time for his last run he waited but the man did not show. Concerned, he sent someone to check the house where the man had gone. They found him lying dead from an apparent heart attack beside his car which was stuck in the sand. The information was relayed back to Snookie and he radioed the Sheriff's office. They asked if he could put the man's body in his car and bring it back to the mainland. He agreed to transport the body and the Sheriff's office said they would be at the Cat Point ferry dock to meet him. When he arrived at the ferry docks there was no deputy to be seen. Snookie had to wait with the body for an hour and a half until they showed up. By then he was mad, and he let them know he did not appreciate having to babysit a dead man. The only other time he brought a body from the Island was when a surf fisherman had been struck and killed by lighting. The Sheriff's office was there to meet him that time.

Teenage girls in bathing suits liked riding with him in the pilot house. One day the ferry was passing by where they were driving pilings for the new bridge, and he asked the girls if they wanted to see how they could stop the pile driver. They asked him "how?" and he told them to stand out on the deck as the ferry passed the pile-driver operator. When the ferry with the two young beauties went by him, the operator stopped his machine to gawk at the girls.

Snookie worked on the St. George Island ferry *Sirius* until it was retired and replaced by a toll bridge in 1965. The Dog Island ferry *Spica* ran until April 30, 1982 when it too was retired. Snookie said he made the last run to St. George Island on December 14, 1965. Because the ferry still had to have a licensed captain aboard, he continued manning the vessel for a couple of months after the bridge had opened. The *Sirius* was eventually sold to a pulpwood company on the Chattahoochee River that used it to ferry lumber trucks across the river. The last time he saw it was when he piloted it to Panama City to be pulled out of the water for repairs before the sale.

Joseph Wesley "Snookie" Barber, 87 years old in 2008, was living in Carrabelle when I spoke with him. He said he liked to ride the woods around the area to see the bears, snakes, otters and deer. Age may have slowed him down a little but he's always willing to spend time talking about the old days. His life contains the history and stories of the area and he knows that soon they will be lost. In his eyes I could still see a proud young man, the Captain of the *Sirius*, greeting tourists, asking how they've been since the last time he saw them and telling the kids to stay away from the rails. Snookie died in 2014 at age 92. I was privileged to be able to speak with him and remember my own childhood ferry trips to St. George.

## Finally, a St. George Island Bridge

In July of 1956 the Franklin County Commission approved a resolution asking the State Road Department to begin engineering and financing studies on constructing a bridge from Cat Point to St. George Island. A similar resolution had been passed in 1952 but no action had been taken. The 30year plan was to finance the bridge with Franklin County secondary road monies and tolls. The State Road Department was asked to determine the best route and feasibility of their financing plan.

It looked like things were finally going to start moving, but it was not until June of 1958 that money for building the bridge was pledged. The Franklin County Commission pledged 80 percent of its fifth and sixth cent gas tax funds for secondary roads for the project. It was expected this would provide three and a half to four million dollars for the project. But by 1960 there was still no bridge.

In September of 1963 the State Road Department announced a proposed design for a bridge that could be built with current funds allocated, approximately $4,080,000. To protect oyster beds and traverse deeper water in the Bay the bridge would curve over the intercoastal waterway channel. In December bids were let for a bond financed bridge to St. George Island. Hardaway Contracting Co. of Columbus, Georgia was awarded the contract for a bid of $3,337,527. The bid called for completion of the bridge within 300 working days.

Developers of St. George contributed another $5000,000 to the amount and Franklin county added a borrowed $235,000 for a total of $3,565,000 available for construction. In an agreement pushed by W.T. Mayo of the State Road Department the developers agreed to deed the east tip of the island to the state for a park. The deal was contingent on the state building a primary road from the bridge to the park within five years from the April 1963 agreement signing. This would give the state three miles of public beach. The state failed to move on the project within the allotted five years and the land for the park was never transferred. In 1973 the state purchased that same land for $6.5 million.

Construction of the bridge began March 30, 1964. By August of 1965 the bridge was 85% complete. Round-trip tolls were set for the bridge with $1.50 for motorcycles, motorbikes and bicycles, $7.00 for buses, two-axel vehicles $2.00, 3-axel $3.00, 4 axel $4.00, semi-trailers $5.00. Because most vehicles using the bridge were two axel it soon was called the "twodollar bridge" by locals. The 3.8- mile St. George Island bridge was opened December 17, 1965 at 7 a.m. without fanfare, but it had opened a new area in the islands and Franklin counties development.

The bridge was formally dedicated and named after the late State Rep Bryant Grady Patton in a September 4, 1967 Labor Day ceremony. A two- mile waiting line of cars sat at the entrance to the bridge during the dedication ceremonies.

When the bridge was opened 1,400 cars crossed over it that first day. On the island the Jaycees held a fish fry and dune buggy race, but the planned sky-diving was cancelled due to high winds. When the bridge opened in 1965 there were 60 private homes on the island and 2,000 lots had already been sold. It had taken 14 years for the bridge to finally be built.

The tolls would continue to be collected until 1992. With better access to the island visitors started coming to spend the weekend or their vacations. Two realtors handled the rental units on the island, Alice B. Collins and H.G. Smith. They offered rentals by night, weekend or week. Costs for an apartment sleeping four to six went from $165 to $360 a week, $95 to $125 for a 2 ½- day weekend, and $25 to $50 a night. Prices dropped by one third after Labor Day.

St. George Island Bridge under construction 1964

## But What About the Dog Island Bridge?

Many had hoped to see a second bridge built to Dog Island. But once the county monies had been allocated for the St. George Bridge it seemed a lost cause. The final nail in its coffin was the passing of state and federal laws in 1985 prohibiting the spending of government money on bridges to barrier islands.

Ferry "Sirius" St. George Schedule

## Improving the Island

Atkinson, Wilson and their partners in the St. George Island Gulf Beaches, Inc. set about improving the island, they also worked to foster goodwill with the County. In 1953 they deeded a half-mile strip of land across the island's western tip for a new channel. The ten-foot deep channel would allow boats quicker access to the gulf, saving a 20 to 30-mile trip. Today that channel is known as the Bob Sikes Channel.

## The Bob Sikes Channel - "The Cut"

1967 Aerial View of Bob Sikes Channel- Florida Memory State Archives

The Bob Sikes Channel, commonly known as the "Cut" was named after former Congressman Roert F. "Bob" Sikes who pushed the legislation through Congress. The honor was bestowed on Sikes by a resolution of the Florida legislature in 1955. The land for the channel was deeded to Franklin Cunty by the St. George Island-Gulf Beach, Inc in July of 1953. In 1953 Franklin County approved the use of county gas tax funds to dig the 10-foot deep, 100-ft wide channel through St. George Island. This was the first time in the history of the state that gasoline tax monies were approved for waterway construction. In the past their use was restricted to highway projects, but the Franklin County delegation got approval through a special act in the legislature. Initial work on the channel was completed by the County in November of 1954. The Army Corps of Engineers were then tasked with the dredging and installation of the jetties. A formal opening and dedication, highlighted by a blast of dynamite in the narrow channel, marked the first step in its complete dredging in June of 1956.

The Cut created a shortcut from Apalachicola to the Gulf of Mexico for local commercial fishermen. Previously it took the fishing fleet four hours to travel twelve miles around the west end of Little St. George. The Cut reduced that time to one hour and also opened up 20 more miles of fishing grounds. The channel was the realization of an idea that had been envisioned as far back as 1890.

The two rock jetties formed a prime fishing location for recreational anglers. Fishermen would travel an old turpentine trail cut in the center of the island in four-wheel vehicles to fish the "rocks" as it was called. When the land surrounding the trail was sold to create the St. George Plantation it became privately owned by the deed holder.

The St. George Island developers continued to promote their holdings. In 1957 they opened the island up to the 750 Boy Scouts to hold their annual Camporee. It was the largest group ever to assemble in the Big Bend. The ferry boats were offered for free transportation and the corporations Island Manager, George Bradford helped to get them to their campsites and provided much of the equipment they needed. A special commemorative St. George Island shoulder patch was presented to each camper.

## ST. GEORGE ISLAND

We have just one 100 x 175 waterfront lot. Price $2,500. Terms $250 down, $50 per month.

**BEAUTIFUL** waterfront lot with high elevation overlooking open Gulf on St. George Island. Price $2500. Small down payment, 5 years on balance.

## BEACH HOMES
### ON ST. GEORGE ISLAND

WE HAVE 2 beautiful beach homes on St. George Island for sale and many outstanding waterfront and water view lots, priced from $500 to $2500. Terms to fit your budget. Call for appointment.

Sale Advertisements for St. George Lots 1957

By 1958 there were 35 completed homes and five more under construction. Seven hundred people had purchased lots on the island. The developers laid out 15 miles of paved and hard surfaced roads, laid out subdivision's and opened a yacht basin for boaters.

Permanent electrical service came to the island in 1958. Florida Power Company ran a power line across the water for a cost of $85,000 to supply the 40 homes on the island. Each subscriber had to pay a minimum $10 a month charge until usage on the island was high enough to go to standard charges. Prior to then, electrical service was provided by a temporary power plant erected by St. George Island Beaches, Inc. Franklin County Commissioners still placed high hopes on the future development of the island and its tax revenues.

In 1950 the property tax rate in Franklin county was $700, but by 1960 it was $15,000. The developers assured the county that by 1970 the island would be responsible for over 50% of the property taxes. In 2004 Franklin county collected $8 million in property taxes. By 2017 the value of all taxable property in Franklin County was $1,825,653,612.00.

After the bridge was built property sales started to move but remained slow with a total of 120 homes built. In 1971 Atkinson and the St. George Island Gulf Beaches Inc. sold most of their holdings to John Stocks and Gene Brown for a $6 million mortgage, $10 million cash and other valuable considerations. Included in the sale's documents was a list of individual owners consisting of 23 limited partners and 33 shareholders of the old St. George Island Gulf Beaches, Inc.

## ST. GEORGE ISLAND LTD

| NAME | AMOUNT |
|---|---|
| Sara A. Rodrigue | $ 5,160.00 |
| Charles Rosenberg, Jr. | 960.00 |
| Frances M. Spottswood | 900.00 |
| Doris L. Belk | 120.00 |
| H. J. Belk | 120.00 |
| Robert C. Parker | 1,800.00 |
| Homer A. Brinkley | 2,700.00 |
| Robert T. Brinkley | 2,700.00 |
| Mary L. Patton | 3,780.00 |
| Sidney W. Mendelson | 1,800.00 |
| Harold D. Mendelson | 1,800.00 |
| Hazel M. Rackleff | 180.00 |
| Mrs. H. M. Stiegler | 720.00 |
| Patricia Wilson Atkinson | 375.00 |
| Harry A. Johnson | 1,800.00 |
| Raymond Diehl, Jr. | 6,900.00 |
| J. David O'Dea | 180.00 |
| Shirley L. O'Dea | 180.00 |
| Miriam Wilson | 180.00 |
| R. L. Wilson | 22,830.00 |
| William H. Wilson | 22,830.00 |
| Byron Block | 5,400.00 |
| Sara Elizabeth Atkinson Rodrigue, as Trustee | 36,585.00 |
| 2nd ADD ST. GEORGE ISLAND .... SHARES | ........ |

List of St. George Investors/Owners 1972

| SHARES | ST. GEORGE ISLAND GULF BEACHES INC. | |
|---|---|---|
| 32.5 | Mrs. Mary L. Patton | $ 195,000.00 |
| 15. | Robert C. Parker | 90,000.00 |
| 15. | Sidney W. Mendelson | 90,000.00 |
| 5. | Harold D. Mendelson | 90,000.00 |
| 15. | Harry A. Johnson | 90,000.00 |
| 72.75 | Clyde W. Atkinson | 436,500.00 |
| 70.375 | Elizabeth C. Atkinson | 422,250.00 |
| 3.125 | Patricia Wilson Atkinson | 18,750.00 |
| 43. | Sara Atkinson Rodrique | 258,000.00 |
| 16.5 | Sara Elizabeth Rodrigue - Trustee | 99,000.00 |
| 45. | Al B. Block | 270,000.00 |
| 22.5 | Homer A. Brinkley | 135,000.00 |
| 22.5 | Robert T. Brinkley | 135,000.00 |
| 57.5 | Estate of Raymond Diehl, Sr. | 345,000.00 |
| 37.5 | R. L. Wilson | 225,000.00 |
| 37.5 | William H. Wilson | 225,000.00 |
| 165.25 | William H. & R. L. Wilson | 991,500.00 |
| 6. | Mrs. H. M. Stiegler | 36,000.00 |
| 1.50 | Hazel M. Rackleff | 9,000.00 |
| 1.50 | Marian Wilson | 9,000.00 |
| 1.50 | J. David O'Dea | 9,000.00 |
| 1.50 | Shirley L. O'Dea | 9,000.00 |
| 7.50 | Frances M. Spottswood | 45,000.00 |
| 2. | H. J. & Doris Belk | 18,000.00 |
| 5. | Southernaire Motel Inc. | 30,000.00 |
| 8. | Charlotte Rosenberg | 48,000.00 |
| 112,833 | Estate of Charles Rosenberg | 676,998.00 |
| 83.333 | S. B. Deeb | 499,998.00 |
| 2.334 | W. Guy McKenzie Sr. | 14,004.00 |
| 27. | J. H. Kennedy, W. Guy McKenzie Jr. & Sara Pat McKenzie, Trustees | 162,000.00 |
| 27. | W. Guy McKenzie Jr. | 162,000.00 |
| 27. | Gayle McKenzie Landrum | 162,000.00 |
| 1000. | | $6,000,000.00 |

List of St. George Investors/Owners 1972

## Gene Brown and John Stocks, Leisure Properties

In 1973 Brown and Stocks Leisure Properties Inc. sold 1,883 acres on the east end of the island to the State of Florida for six and a half million dollars. The state developed the property into a state park called the Dr. Julian G. Bruce St. George Island State Park. Dr. Bruce was a dentist and former Franklin County Commissioner. The island slowly began to grow, but sales still lagged. It took almost a year for the developers to sell the first two miles of lots. They were offering five-acre beach front lots for $45,000 apiece. The men had big plans to develop the island wanting to build 40,000 condominiums but ran into opposition from a protective Franklin County Commission. The Commission feared a major development would pollute the bay and adversely affect seafood production. Wanting to limit lot sizes, density, and height restrictions for any buildings, they fought any zoning requests to the contrary. It would be a nine-year battle the developers would never win. In 1974 they got approval to build a single-family subdivision calling it the St. George Plantation. But they still had plans for multi-family structures and commercial development on a 33-acre piece of gulf front property called "Sunset Beach" near the state park and a 40-acre tract in the middle of the island. In 1978 the Commission tried to rewrite their zoning laws prohibiting high-density structures in the middle portion of the island, then required houses to be built on pilings in lower areas but lost the battle in court. Stocks and Brown's partnership would dissolve in 1981 with Brown keeping Leisure Properties.

## The St. George Plantation

In 1981 Brown developed 1, 200 acres on the westernmost end of the island calling it the St. George Plantation, a private gated community with an airstrip. Brown also built and owns the St. George Island Utility Company that supplies the islands drinking water.

**Gene Brown**

Advertisement for Lots at the Plantation

## Access Through the Plantation to Cut Becomes an Issue

Access to the Cut had been a bone of contention since 1977 when the St. George Plantation was established. A state Development of Regional Impact (DRI) order required the

Association to allow public access to the Cut. It also required for 10 public parking spaces to be provided. The only access to "The Cut" through the St. George Plantation was on a private road called Leisure Lane. Developer Gene Brown initially allowed fishermen to drive through the plantation to fish but in 1985 he closed the road to public traffic. Due to criticism from fishermen and County Commissioners, he reopened it in 1987 charging each vehicle $5 to drive to the Cut. He later turned control of the road to the Homeowners Association who upped the price to $6 a person.

Homeowners contended that access had been granted as a "privilege" for 20 years, but in 1996 they voted to close the road through their subdivision to the public entirely, citing liability concerns. They said they did not want to be liable if a fisherman hurt himself on the jetties or had a vehicle accident on the property. Homeowners reasoned it had always their intention to cut off access when the area became more developed. The creation of the new Schooner Landing subdivision gave them an excuse. That left the only access to the Cut by boat. Many fishermen were disappointed in their decision saying the Cut was built with public funds and should be accessible.

But they had little recourse since the road was a private road under the Associations control and they could still access it by boat. In 1999 the issue was raised again but the county, which would be responsible for enforcing the DRI (and assuming liability), chose not to get involved. Today land access is limited to homeowners and rental customers in the St. George Plantation. A parking area outside the Schooner Landing community is provided with a pathway allowing access to the beach and jetty.

## A New St. George Island Bridge

The first island bridge was replaced forty years later. The replacement bridge was opened/dedicated February 27, 2004 and the name Bryant Grady Patton bridge was retained. The new bridge had wider lanes and emergency pull-off areas that the first did not. To allow for commercial boat traffic to pass, it rises 65 feet at its highest point. The 4.1- mile bridge is the third longest bridge in Florida after the Seven Mile Bridge in the Florida Keys and the 5.5-mile Sunshine Skyway Bridge over Tampa Bay.

The old bridge was demolished but six tenths of a mile on both ends were left as fishing piers. The middle area, which was a nesting habitat for birds, was left in place.

## Cape St. George- Little St. George Lighthouse

The first lighthouse was built in 1833 on the extreme western tip of the island marking the entrance to Apalachicola Bay. It was 65 feet tall with 13 lamps. The height of the lighthouse proved to be too low, with the light often being blocked by trees on the point. It was replaced by a second new 15 lamp lighthouse in 1848.

An 1850 hurricane cracked and undermined the tower and another 1851 hurricane toppled it. In 1852 a 72-foot tower using bricks from ruins of the old tower was built 250 yards inland from the old tower and 552 yards from the Gulf. The light was extinguished in 1861 with the start of the Civil War.

It was relit in 1865. A new lighthouse keepers building was built in 1878 but was damaged by waves from another hurricane washing over the island. The light was lit with mineral oil in 1882 and then incandescent oil vapor in 1913.

Cape St. George Lighthouse 1930s

The keepers house burned down in the 1940s. In October of 1949 the lighthouse was made automatic, no longer needing a keeper.

The Cape was separated from the main island with the development of the Bob Skies Cut in 1957 and is now known as Little St. George. In July of 1994 the Coast Guard removed the light.

The lighthouse fell into disrepair and was being undermined by encroachment of the gulf. In 1982 the lighthouse had stood 150 yards from the shoreline and was protected by four sand dunes. Hurricanes Kate and Elena in 1985 destroyed much of the protecting dune lines and waves were soon washing at its base

Hurricane Opal in 1995 washed out most of the foundation causing it to lean precariously at a 10 to 15- degree angle. By 1997 waves were lapping at its base. A non-profit group calling itself the Cape St. George Lighthouse Society sprang

into action raising monies and securing grants to restore the light. A company was hired to fix the foundation. Twenty holes were drilled around its base then filled with fiberglass bars and concrete. The bars were then attached to a ring of concrete. That base was placed on 20 wooden pilings, each sunk 15 feet in the ground. The entire structure was then surrounded by a circular concrete filled seawall sunk 10 feet in the ground. In 1999 their efforts were further challenged by the U.S. government that was considering selling it and five other Florida lighthouses to pay for Everglades cleanup. A historical grant had been sought to move the lighthouse to a safer more accessible location, but Hurricane Dennis struck on July 10, 2005 further undermining the lighthouse.

Lighthouse after Hurricane's Opal

The Cape St. George Lighthouse that had stood for 153 years finally collapsed at 11:45 a.m. on October 21, 2005. Today the Cape where it had stood it is part of the Apalachicola National Estuarine Research Reserve.

Undeterred, a non-profit citizens support group called the St. George Lighthouse Association set about collecting the debris to use in its restoration. In 2008 the dismantled lighthouse was rebuilt to a height of 79 feet. It now stands in the center of the main island, fourteen miles from its original location on Little St. George.

A Lighthouse Keepers House Museum and gift shop were formally opened in August of 2011. Begun in 2009 and completed in 2010, the two-story building is a replica of the first lighthouse keepers house built on Little St. George in 1852.

## Indian Pass

Located on the eastern end of Franklin County, Indian Pass is 8 miles south of Port St. Joe. The name refers to the natural pass leading from the Apalachicola Bay to the Gulf of Mexico. The area is famous for its great raw oysters. If you are from Tallahassee you have often heard a commercial that says *"You Know Where...* then names a local restaurant. But if you have ever traveled down to the Forgotten Coast for oysters, the rest of that sentence would be ...*The Indian Pass Raw Bar.* It is located on County Road 30A ten minutes southeast of Port St. Joe, Fl.

The McNeil's, a pioneer Gulf county family, have run a popular raw bar at Indian Pass for the past thirty-five years. The building housing the raw bar is an old turpentine commissary-company store built in 1903 and had served as the McNeil's wholesale oyster business. The raw bar did not begin operations until 1986 after Hurricane Kate blew through town. It features oysters, beer and music and is popular to bikers and yuppies alike. A weathered painting of an Indian chief looks out from atop the store.

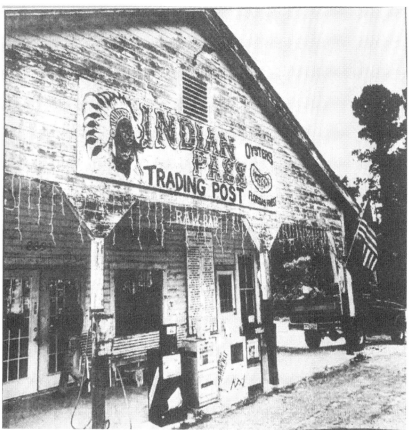

The Indian Pass Raw Bar

# St Vincent Island

**Aerial view of St. Vincent Island**

St. Vincent island is triangular shaped and contains some 12,358 acres of wetlands, dunes, and pines. It is four miles wide on the east end and nine miles long. West Pass separates it from Little St. George on the east. The west end opens to Indian Pass. There is proof of habitants on the island as far back as 240 A.D. Apalachee, Creek and Seminole Indians once lived there. The island was named by Franciscan Friars in 1633 after the fourth century martyr St. Vincent of Zaragossa.

**St. Vincent of Zaragossa**

The *Apalachicola Land Company* sold St. Vincent to Colonel Robert J. Floyd in 1858. Floyd was a prominent Apalachicola lawyer and father-in-law to Sarah Gorrie Floyd, daughter of inventor Dr. John Gorrie. During the Civil War the island was home to a Confederate fort called Fort Mallory. In 1868 it was bought by Colonel George Hatch at public auction for $3,000. Hatch died on the island in 1875 and his is the only marked grave on the island. It was briefly owned by Francis Avery who sold it back to Mrs. Hatch in 1887. Mrs. Hatch sold 10 acres on the island to the U.S. government for a lighthouse site. On June 12, 1890 the remainder of the island was sold to former Confederate General Edward P. Alexander, former artillery commander in the Army of Northern Virginia during the Civil War and president of the Georgia Central Railroad. Upon Alexander's death the island was bought in 1907 for $12,500 by Dr. Ray Vaughn Pierce.

Pierce was known for his patent medicine business. Many of his cures were aimed at female illnesses and included alcohol and opium. He manufactured "Doctor Pierce's Favorite Prescription," Smart Weed, and Dr. Pierce's Pleasant Pills selling millions of bottles a year. He also authored a book called *"The Peoples Common Sense Medical Advisor in Plain English."*

**Dr. Ray V. Pierce**

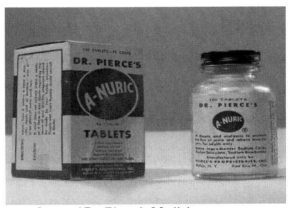

**Some of Dr. Pierce's Medicines**

Using the island as a winter retreat, Pierce established a private hunting preserve stocked with animals from Europe. When Pierce purchased the island, it contained feral hogs thought to have been there since the first European settlers arrived in the area. Pierce upgraded their quality by releasing domestic stock on the island. At a cost of some $50,000 he laid out 30 miles of roads and paths and built dams and cottages on the island. He also raised beef cattle for sale in Apalachicola.

**Dr. Pierce with a wild hog killed on St. Vincent Island**

Pierce died on the island in February of 1914. His estate later sold the first pine saw timber rights to the St. Joe Lumber Company. The company later built a temporary bridge at the refuges 14 -mile site (called the Kenny Mill Bridge) to remove the timber.

In 1923 William Lee Popham purchased an option on the island with the intentions to capitalize on the game preserve. He planned a thousand room club house and hotel accommodations for visiting members. Due to financial difficulties from defending himself of mail fraud charges, nothing ever came of his plans.

Miami developer Vernon Price-Williams bought the island during the Florida land boom of 1925-26 with intentions of developing the island, but the boom collapsed, saving it from development. Price-Williams then sold the land in 1927 to the Big Four Investment Company. The Pierce estate never received their payment for the island, so they contested the sale. A five-year controversy over ownership resulted in the land being sold at public auction in 1932. The Pierce estate bought back the island. Price-Williams committed suicide in 1932 by ingesting poison.

In 1948 the Pierce estate sold the island to Henry and Alfred Lee Loomis, Jr. for $140,000. They were the sons of Alfred Loomis Sr. an attorney, investment banker, scientist and physicist. Alfred Sr. invented the LORAN navigation system which was originally known as "LRN" for Loomis Radio Navigation. In 1934 he purchased an island called Hilton Head. The brothers loved to hunt and used to go to the island to shoot ducks. When their father sold Hilton Head in 1945, the brothers decided to buy their own island and turn it into a private hunting preserve. They imported sambar deer, zebras, elands, Indian antelope, ring-neck pheasants, Asian junglefowl, quail and turkeys to St. Vincent Island. They also upgraded the quality of the swine stock by releasing domestic Brown Russian and Poland China hogs on the island.

**Alfred "Lee "Loomis, Jr.**    **Henry Loomis**

Alfred "Lee" Loomis Jr. was a lawyer, venture capitalist, sailor, and Olympic champion having won a gold medal in the 1948 Olympics in the 6 metre class. Henry Loomis worked for the U.S government, serving as Director of the

Voice of America and Deputy Director of the U.S. Information agency. Later Henry would become President of the Corporation for Public Broadcasting. When the Loomis brothers decided to sell the island in 1968 they wanted it to be kept in its natural state. Shunning developers plans for condos, they instead they sold the island to the Nature Conservancy for $2.2 million. At the time it was one of the largest purchases for the Conservancy.

The Conservancy in turn sold it to the U.S. Fish and Wildlife Service. By using monies from the sales of Duck Stamps, the Wildlife Service repaid them for the island and established the St. Vincent National Wildlife Refuge. With the takeover by the U.S. Fish and Wildlife Service all the exotic animals except the Sambar deer and feral hogs were removed. Today there are swamp buggy tours of the island. The island can be accessed by a boat ferry at the Indian Pass boat ramp. Visitors are also allowed to come to the island by personal boat.

**Shuttle at St. Vincent Island**

At the Indian Pass boat ramp off C30B, a ferry will take tourists across the waterway to St. Vincent Island. Tourists go to the island to take the swamp buggy tour in hopes of spotting the exotic animals located there.

## Cape San Blas

View of Cape San Blas and the St Joseph Peninsula

The Cape has been identified by many names through the years. Maps of the area show it as San Blas in 1722, C.S. Blaise in 1749, Cape Escondido (meaning hidden cape) in 1760, Cape St. Biagio in 1763, and Cape St. Blas in 1787. Other spellings were C. San Blasé and Cape Blaise.

Cape San Blas was named after a Kemetian Bishop who was deported by Constantius, Emperor of Rome (293-306 A.D.) for fighting for and preaching the Nicene Creed. The area was originally called Cape San Plaise. Cape San Blas, a 20-mile peninsula, is made up of two parts. If you were to think of the area as your left arm, the Cape runs from the shoulder at Indian Pass to the elbow (Stump Hole), then the forearm is the St. Joe Peninsula which runs to the mouth of the Bay.

Four lighthouses have been built on the Cape. The first was built in 1849 but was destroyed by a hurricane in 1851. Another lighthouse was erected in 1857 but suffered damages from the Confederates in the Civil War. To protect the lens and tools from the Confederates, they were removed and hidden in Apalachicola; the lighthouse was returned to service in 1865. Erosion soon threatened so it was decided in 1890 to erect a 98-foot tower 1500 feet further inland.

**1890 Lighthouse**

Once again erosion threatened the new tower. Initial plans were to move the light to Blacks Island, but it did not offer high enough visibility off shore. It was decided to move it a quarter mile inland in 1918, where it stood until 2014. The lighthouse was deactivated from service as a navigational aid in 1996.

**View of Eroded Beach**

**Lighthouse and Keepers Cottage 2006**

The Air Force allowed the keeper cottages to be restored in

1998 and both the lighthouse and restored keepers cottages served as a tourist spot. Tourists could go once a month, on a full moon, to climb the tower and view the gulf and St. Joe Bay. Erosion continued to threaten the lighthouse and it was decided to move it to a safer location. On July 15, 2014 it was moved to George Core Park in Port St. Joe.

## St. Joseph Bay

There are many jewels on the Forgotten Coast, but St. Joseph's Bay is the crown jewel, named as early as 1562 by Spanish explorers after Joseph, husband of the Virgin Mary, mother of Jesus.

Though the Spanish ruled Florida, it was the French who built and occupied a fort on the banks of St. Joseph's Bay in May of 1718. Coming into the Bay, they constructed a stockade on the main land across from St. Joseph's Point. The fort was called Fort Crevecoeur which is French for broken heart. I can imagine that was how the soldiers stationed there felt so far away from home.

Soon the Spanish governor of Pensacola protested their intrusion. He sent a ship to take the fort and run the French out of Florida. The French Colonial Council decided the fort was not worth fighting over and abandoned it, after burning it to the ground. The Spanish sailed into the bay on August 20, 1718 and rebuilt the fort, but it too was later abandoned. This ended the brief occupation of St. Joseph Bay by the French. A marker signifying the location of the fort can be found at St. Joe Beach on U.S. 98 at Columbus Street.

The clear pristine waters, not influenced by any freshwater inflow, teem with schools of mullet, redfish, flounder and trout. Sea turtles glide through the water as ancient horseshoe crabs bury themselves on the sandy shores and scallops hide in the sea grasses. Fishermen come year-round to fish these waters. During the July-September scallop season, boaters launch their vessels at Simmons Bayou and the city boat ramp near Maddox Park.

Commercial fishermen guide recreational fishermen in the off-season, then during the mullet and pompano runs in the fall, they turn their attention to the more serious business of making a living. Eco-tours have become popular. One can rent a kayak or canoe and spend the day on the bay paddling out to Blacks Island to see the rusty cannons or along the shore to take pictures of baby eaglets in their nests. The bay, most of which has become an aquatic preserve, supports them all.

### Port St. Joe, A Mill Town

The town of Port St. Joseph was established in 1909. By an act of the legislature the town's name was changed to Port St. Joe on March 10, 1910. From 1938 until its closing in 1998, Port St. Joe was identified by the St. Joe Paper Company mill owned by the DuPont family and run by Edward Ball. Located on the Bay just after one crosses over into North Port St. Joe, it was the major employer in Gulf County. The smell of the mill coupled with chemical odors from the Arizona Chemical plant located just across the street would literally take your breath away if the wind was blowing in your direction.

Most of the town's people were employed by the mill and the jobs paid well. A generation of families worked at the mill and their children looked forward to careers there as well. Most of the local businesses needed the mill to balance their cost sheets. Pulpwood truck drivers, and multiple banks located on the main road coming into town relied on their steady business. The town moved to the rhythm of the mill shift changes. Workers clocked in or out to shifts that rotated every 30 days. The demise of the mill started innocently enough, in 1996 there was a shut down that many thought would only last a week. The days stretched out until it was announced the mill had been sold to Florida Coast Paper. They operated the mill until the decline of the container board market made it unprofitable to continue. The mill was shut down August 16, 1998. By 2003 the mill had been dismantled and a piece of Forgotten Coast history passed away into memories.

**St. Joe Paper Co. Mill in Port St. Joe**

## Mexico Beach

When the European's came to its shores, the area was inhabited by Apalachee Indians. The beach area on the eastern tip of Bay County was slow to develop. In the 1830s travelers passed through on Public Road #64, a sand road known as the Old Stage Road. The road was connected to St. Andrews Bay and went to the port city of Apalachicola.

Around 1901 Felix Du Pont bought the property that is todays Mexico Beach to harvest the pine trees and naval stores. Highway 98, which followed the footprint of the Old Stage Road, was completed in 1937 and people began to take notice of the miles of white sand beach. Tyndall Air Force Base was built in 1941 and soon the soldiers were coming there to enjoy the beach and relax.

In 1946 developers Gordon Parker, W.T. McGowin Sr. and J.W. Wainwright bought 1,850 acres of beachfront property for $65,000. In 1948 they named the area Mexico Beach due to its proximity to the Gulf of Mexico. A canal was cut in 1955 giving the approximately 200 residents access to the

Gulf. The town of Mexico Beach was incorporated in 1967. Known for its old Florida lifestyle, there were no traffic lights in the town. Mexico Beach soon became a favorite for fishermen and beachgoers.

By the year 2018 there were about 1,000 residents and it was labeled the "Unforgettable Coast." The name meant even more when on October 10, 2018 Hurricane Michael came roaring ashore as a Category Five Hurricane with 160 mph winds. It destroyed nearly all of the homes and businesses. Today its residents are still trying to recover. If you would like to help, check out neverforgottencoast.com for information about assisting their recovery through micro-grants.

Coppertone was the lotion of choice in the Sixties

## CHAPTER SIX – GETTING THERE NOW

Roll down your windows, smell the salt air and feel the warm sunshine. Tune your radio to *WOYS Oyster Radio 100.5 FM "The Voice of the Forgotten Coast,"* turn the music up loud and let your worries slip away. You are now cruising in the Forgotten Coast!

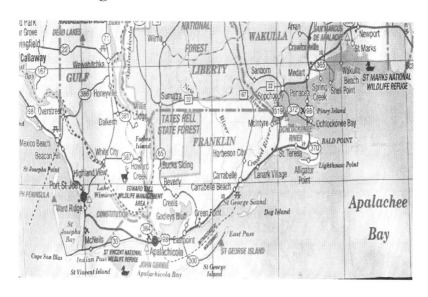

**San Marcos de Apalache State Park:** 148 Old Fort Rd, St. Marks, Fl

**St. Marks Lighthouse**: located six miles from the Fort in the St. Marks National Wildlife Refuge.
From Tallahassee, take SR 363 (Woodville Hwy) to Wakulla. Turn left (east) on SR 267 (Bloxham Cutoff). At US 98 (Coastal Hwy), turn left (east) and cross the St. Marks River. Turn right on Lighthouse Road (CR 59).
www.fws.gov/saintmarks   GPS: 84° 10.955' W- 30° 4.65' N

**Wakulla Beach:** Wakulla Beach Road is located off Hwy 98, 3.5 miles west of St. Marks on your left as you head west, follow the road to its end at the Gulf. 30°06'33"N 84°15'33"W

**Shell Point:** Lies at the end of County Road 367 in Wakulla County. Turn south onto County Road 365 from U.S. Hwy 98 and then onto County road 367. 27°52'47"N 82°29'02"W

**Panacea, Fl:** 30°01'53"N 84°23'37"W

**Ochlocknee Point:** Is at the end of County Road 372 off U.S. 98 in Wakulla County. Turn left on County road 372 at the blinking light just before the bridge south of Panacea. Area is also known as Mashes Sands.

**Bald Point State Park**: 146 Cut Box Road, Alligator Point. www.baldpointstatepark.com

**Alligator Point:** South of Panacea after crossing the Ochlocknee Bay bridge on U.S. 98 turn onto County Road 370 . As you travel out the peninsula, Alligator Point is to the right, Bald Point is to the left.

**Old Wakulla County Courthouse** 23 High Drive Crawfordville, Fl

**Lanark Village:** Located off Highway 98, Five miles east of Carrabelle, FL 29°53'0"N 84°35'45"W

**Carrabelle, Fl:** On Hwy 98 29°51'14"N 84°39'57"W

**Camp Gordon Johnston WWII Museum**: 1873 Highway 98 West in Carrabelle, Fl www.campgordonjohston.com
**Crooked River Lighthouse**: Approximately two miles west

142

of the Carrabelle bridge at 1975 Highway 98 West. Traveling west from Carrabelle look for brown Historical Marker sign on north side of Highway. www.crookedriverlighthouse.org

**Eastpoint, Fl:** 29°44'30"N 84°52'37"W

**St. George Island:** 29.659°N 84.878°W

**Cape St. George Light:** Located at the center of St. George Island. From U.S. 98 in Eastpoint turn onto state road 300 (Island Drive) and cross the 4.2 -mile bridge to St. George Island.

**Apalachicola:** on Hwy    9829°43'31"N 84°59'33"W

**Indian Pass Raw Bar** is located at 8391 Country Road 30A at intersection of 30A & 30B in Gulf County, FL

**Indian Pass** is located eight miles south of Port St. Joe, Fl. Turn onto C-30B at the Indian Pass Raw Bar and follow the road to its end to the Indian Pass Campground. St. Vincent Island is located across the water accessible by a daily ferry. GPS: 29°41'25" North, 85°15'51" West

**St. Vincent Island** Visitor center located in the Harbor Master Building on north end of Market Street in Apalachicola. To get to island take U.S Highway 98 west to County Rd 30A. Turn at Indian Pass Raw Bar, follow road to Indian Pass. Shuttle (850) 229-1065.

**Cape San Blas:** Turn left off of 30A. Located 10 miles S-SW of Port St. Joe 29°39'49"N 85°21'20"W.

143

**Cape San Blas Light:** Located in downtown Port St. Joe in the George Core Park. Take U.S. 98 west to Port St. Joe light is on your left after you come through the intersection of U.S. 98 and state road 71.   29°40'16.41"N 85°21'22.72"W

**Mexico Beach:**  On Hwy 98 25 miles south of Panama City, Fl 29°56'29"N 85°24'23"

## When you go be sure to visit:

St. Marks **Lighthouse** and **Old Fort** -check out the alligators, eagles, and migrating monarch butterflies. Stop and eat at **Ouzts' Too**.

Wakulla Beach view the ruins of the **old hotel**.

Crawfordville Visit the **Old Courthouse** and the **Wakulla County Historical Museum** located in the old jail.

Medart - be sure to  stop at **Rocky's** for food and drinks or go to **Hutton's Seafood** for the fresh catch of the day.

Panacea- the old **Panacea Mineral Springs** across from the **Welcome Center, Mineral Springs Seafood** to buy some smoked mullet. Visit the **Gulf Specimen Marine Lab**.

Bald Point **State Park**.

Summer Camp- view the beautiful coast.

Lanark- **Lanark Market**

Carrabelle –**The Junction,** the **World's Smallest Police**

Station, the **Bottle House, Crooked River Lighthouse** and **Camp Gordon Johnston WWII Museum at Carrabelle Beach.**

St. George Island – Eat at the **Blue Parrot,** visit the **Lighthouse** and **Dr. Julian Bruce State Park**.

Apalachicola- the **Downtown Books and Purl** and the **Grady Market.** Take Hwy98 to **30A** the **Scenic Route** to Indian Pass.

Indian Pass – Visit the **Indian Pass Raw Bar** and eat some oysters then ride down to **Indian Pass** and look over at **St. Vincent Island.**

Cape San Blas- take the drive out to the **T.H. Stone Memorial State Park.**

Port St. Joe - visit the **Lighthouse, Constitution Museum,** and eat at the **Marina.** While in the area go up Hwy 71 to Wewahitchka and get some tupelo honey at **Smiley's.**

Mexico Beach see the ruins from Hurricane Michael and stop at **Al Cathey's Ace Hardware** and make a donation to help the folks hurt by the terrible storm.

**Want to learn more about the Forgotten Coast? Check out some of my other books:**

**Remembering Florida's Forgotten Coast**

**The Florida Seafood Cookbook**

**These and others are available on Amazon, Lulu.com, and Barnes & Nobles.**

Fire Tower at The St. Marks Lighthouse Refuge

Made in the USA
Columbia, SC
21 June 2021